Turtles

OUR BEST FRIENDS

OUR BEST FRIENDS

Turtles

Marie Devers

ELDORADO INK

Produced by OTTN Publishing, Stockton, New Jersey

Eldorado Ink
PO Box 100097
Pittsburgh, PA 15233
www.eldoradoink.com

First printing

1 3 5 7 9 8 6 4 2

Library of Congress Cataloging-in-Publication Data

Devers, Marie.
  Turtles / Marie Devers.
      p. cm. — (Our best friends)
  ISBN 978-1-932904-34-5 (hardcover) — ISBN 978-1-932904-42-0 (trade edition)
  1. Turtles—Juvenile literature. I. Title.
  QL666.C5D46 2008
  597.92—dc22

                        2008033061

Photo credits: Courtesy of Clunio: 28; Courtesy Michael J. Coscia: 53, 77, 79 (both), 92, 97,
99; © 2008 Jupiterimages Corporation: 3; Courtesy Jason C. Price: 49 (both), 60, 80; Used
under license from Shutterstock, Inc.: 8, 11, 13, 16, 18 (both), 20, 22, 25, 26, 29, 31, 33, 35,
36, 38, 41, 43, 44, 46, 51, 56, 57, 58, 63, 64, 66, 68, 69, 70, 73, 82, 86, 91, 93, 95,
"Fun Fact" icon image, front cover (all), back cover; Courtesy Johnathan Zander: 23;
© iStockphoto.com/Christian Nasca: 89.

TABLE OF CONTENTS

Introduction

GARY KORSGAARD, DVM

The mutually beneficial relationship between humans and animals began long before the dawn of recorded history. Archaeologists believe that humans began to capture and tame wild goats, sheep, and pigs more than 9,000 years ago. These animals were then bred for specific purposes, such as providing humans with a reliable source of food or providing furs and hides that could be used for clothing or the construction of dwellings.

Other animals had been sought for companionship and assistance even earlier. The dog, believed to be the first animal domesticated, began living and working with Stone Age humans in Europe more than 14,000 years ago. Some archaeologists believe that wild dogs and humans were drawn together because both hunted the same prey. By taming and training dogs, humans became more effective hunters. Dogs, meanwhile, enjoyed the social contact with humans and benefited from greater access to food and warm shelter. Dogs soon became beloved pets as well as trusted workers. This can be seen from the many artifacts depicting dogs that have been found at ancient sites in Asia, Europe, North America, and the Middle East.

The earliest domestic cats appeared in the Middle East about 5,000 years ago. Small wild cats were probably first attracted to human settlements because plenty of rodents could be found wherever harvested grain was stored. Cats played a useful role in hunting and killing these pests, and it is likely that grateful humans rewarded them for this assistance. Over time, these small cats gave up some of their aggressive wild behaviors and began living among humans. Cats eventually became so popular in ancient Egypt that they were believed to possess magical powers. Cat statues were placed outside homes to ward off evil spirits, and mummified cats were included in royal tombs to accompany their owners into the afterlife.

Today, few people believe that cats have supernatural powers, but most pet owners feel a magical bond with their pets, whether they are dogs, cats, hamsters, rabbits, horses, or parrots. The lives of pets and their people become inextricably intertwined, providing strong emotional and physical rewards for both humans and animals. People of all ages can benefit from the loving companionship of a pet. Not surprisingly, then, pet ownership is widespread. Recent statistics indicate that about 60 percent of all households in the United States and Canada have at least one pet, while the figure is close to 50 percent of households in the United Kingdom. For millions of people, therefore, pets truly have become their "best friends."

Finding the best animal friend can be a challenge, however. Not only are there many types of domesticated pets, but each has specific needs, characteristics, and personality traits. Even within a category of pets, such as dogs, different breeds will flourish in different surroundings and with different treatment. For example, a German Shepherd may not be the right pet for a person living in a cramped urban apartment; that person might be better off caring for a smaller dog like a Toy Poodle or Shih Tzu, or perhaps a cat. On the other hand, an active person who loves the outdoors may prefer the companion-ship of a Labrador Retriever to that of a small dog or a passive indoor pet like a goldfish or hamster.

The joys of pet ownership come with certain responsibilities. Bringing a pet into your home and your neighborhood obligates you to care for and train the pet properly. For example, a dog must be housebroken, taught to obey your commands, and trained to behave appropriately when he encounters other people or animals. Owners must also be mindful of their pet's particular nutritional and medical needs.

The purpose of the OUR BEST FRIENDS series is to provide a helpful and comprehensive introduction to pet ownership. Each book contains the basic information a prospective pet owner needs in order to choose the right pet for his or her situation and to care for that pet throughout the pet's lifetime. Training, socialization, proper nutrition, potential medical issues, and the legal responsibilities of pet ownership are thoroughly explained and discussed, and an abundance of expert tips and suggestions are offered. Whether it is a hamster, corn snake, guinea pig, or Labrador Retriever, the books in the OUR BEST FRIENDS series provide everything the reader needs to know about how to have a happy, well-adjusted, and well-behaved pet.

Turtles are fascinating creatures and many people enjoy watching them. Turtles like the red-eared slider (opposite) make great pets because they adapt well to captivity.

CHAPTER ONE

Is a Turtle Right for You?

Turtles have been walking the earth for a long time! Scientists have found turtle fossils that are more than 200 million years old. These fossils date back long before birds and mammals existed. The fossils show that turtles roamed the earth at the same time that dinosaurs did. Although dinosaurs no longer exist, turtles are still thriving.

The earth's climate was much warmer when dinosaurs were alive. Turtles today have the same physical characteristics that they had millions of years ago, so they feel most comfortable in warm climates. Turtles are ectotherms, which means that external conditions raise or lower their body temperature. To warm up, turtles must bask in the sun; to cool down, they can go for a swim. This is why most turtles in the wild live in warm places. However, many types of turtles have adjusted to living in parts of the world that have cold seasons. Turtles have been able to survive changes to their habitats by evolving. Some species of turtles can now hibernate through cold winters.

Over 200 types of turtles exist today. Turtles live in all sorts of places and come in all shapes and sizes—from the size of a quarter to the size of a small car! Today's turtles fall into two groups. Cryptodirans have shorter necks, which they can retract into their shells. Pleurodirans, on the other hand, wrap their long necks along the side of their shells.

GOOD HOMES FOR PET TURTLES

Turtles can make fun pets, but they are also a big responsibility. In the wild, turtles can take care of their own needs. When you take a turtle as a pet, you have to commit to caring for all the turtle's needs.

Children can make great turtle owners, as long as the adults in their lives help them make sure everything is being done to properly care for the turtle. Remember that taking care of a pet turtle can be demanding, so if your turtle's care is primarily a child's responsibility, please make it your responsibility to ensure that the turtle is getting everything it needs.

BEING A GOOD TURTLE OWNER

First and foremost, turtle owners must learn all that they can about their new pets. The fact that you are reading this book is a good sign that you are just the kind of person who will make a great turtle owner.

Your turtle's most basic needs are the same as your own. Turtles need food, shelter, and water. Every species of turtle has different requirements in each of these areas. The specific needs of different types of turtles are discussed later in this book.

Even if you do not have a large yard, your turtle can still have plenty of room to roam. Turtles require only a small amount of space. You do not need an exotic pet store nearby to keep a turtle, either. Most basic pet stores, and even some supermarkets, sell all the supplies you'll need to feed and care for your turtle.

Turtles have been known to get along well with adult dogs, but if you have a frisky puppy, you may want to wait a few years for the puppy to calm down before you get a pet turtle. Watch all dogs around your pet turtle. Do not allow dogs—no matter how trustworthy—to be alone with your turtle until you are sure the dog will not hurt the turtle.

Turtles make great pets for people who want to sit back and observe them. Turtles do not play fetch, and most do not like to be held. Although turtles are known for their hard

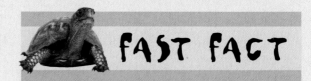

FAST FACT

Turtles often catch flack for being slow, but their hard shells make moving fast impossible. Turtles do not need to move fast because most turtles are vegetarians, so they do not have to hunt other animals, and they simply retreat into their shells if they are under attack.

Be sure to watch your turtle's interactions with other animals to ensure his safety.

shells, they are delicate living creatures. They will not be happy in a home where children or adults roughhouse with them. Turtles do not deal well with stress. Turtles scare very easily, and when they are scared they will retreat into their shells.

IS A TURTLE THE RIGHT PET FOR YOU?

If you are looking for a lively pet that will greet you at the door when you come home from work, you might want to reconsider getting a pet turtle. While some turtle owners report that their pets notice them when they walk into a room, many more owners say their turtles are rather aloof creatures.

Some turtle owners claim that their pets scamper to the edge of their terrariums when they approach. Other owners have reported that their turtles stretch out their legs and try to reach up when their owners peek into their tanks. Very few turtles have learned to do tricks. Although all these things could happen, do not be alarmed if your turtle pays no attention to you whatsoever.

AN ARTIST TURTLE

Koopa is a painting turtle who lives in Hartford Connecticut. He is now retired, but during his five-year career, he painted over 800 works of art! Of course, Koopa did not do all of the work. First, his owner, artist Kira Ayn Varszegi, would spread special nontoxic paint onto a large canvas. Then Koopa would use his shell and feet to "paint" the colors into an abstract design. Koopa's paintings hang in all fifty states, and some have sold on eBay for $1,000 or more. Koopa has been featured on *Ripley's Believe It or Not!* and in *USA Today*, and he has his own MySpace page and Web site (www.turtlekiss.com).

Turtles amuse themselves, and they are most interesting to people who simply enjoy observing them.

One way that turtles differ from most pets is in their life span. Turtles have been known to live 20, 50, or even 100 years. Your turtle will most likely rely on you for a long time, so be sure you can commit many years to your turtle.

If you have always wanted a pet but you suffer from allergies, a turtle may be just what you are looking for, as turtles do not shed or trigger human allergies. This is because they do not produce dander—skin and hair particles that prompt most allergic reactions to dogs and cats. For this reason, very few humans are allergic to turtles. If you do suffer from what seems like an allergic reaction after getting a turtle, you are probably reacting to something other than the turtle, such as its food or something in its terrarium.

TERRESTRIAL, AQUATIC, AND SEMI-AQUATIC TURTLES

You can choose a turtle that lives on land (a terrestrial turtle), a turtle that lives in water (an aquatic turtle), or a turtle that lives partly on land and partly in water (a semi-aquatic turtle). Turtles come in all shapes and sizes, so you should become aware of the different types of turtles and their characteristics before choosing one as a pet. You do not

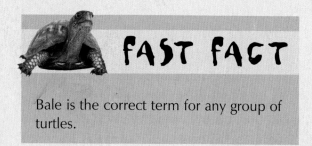

FAST FACT

Bale is the correct term for any group of turtles.

want to fall in love with a two-inch-long (five-cm-long) baby alligator snapping turtle only to learn that it will actually grow to be twelve times its original size in a few years.

BEST ENVIRONMENTS FOR TURTLES

Creating a fun environment is one of the most enjoyable parts of having a turtle. Turtle owners get to create a wonderland for the pets they love. Chapter 4 will give you more in-depth instructions for creating a turtle enclosure.

A cardboard box does not make a good long-term home for a turtle. For terrestrial turtles, you need to buy or build a terrarium. A terrarium is like an aquarium, but it is designed for animals that do not live solely in water. You can buy a terrarium in a pet supply store. Terrariums are made of glass, which provides turtle owners with a nice view of their pets.

Aquatic turtles are more active than terrestrial turtles are, so they require bigger tanks. Because aquatic turtles are more active, however, you will have more turtle activity to watch. You can even add aquatic plants to your aquarium for your turtle to play with and eat. You might find it advantageous to provide a separate feeding tank for your pet. That way, you will not have to clean

Aquatic turtles require more maintenance and equipment than terrestrial turtles. Aquatic turtles need larger tanks, and possibly a separate cage in which to feed.

out your turtle's main living quarters every time it eats.

Outdoor living is great for turtles and even better for their owners, since outside turtle pens are easy to clean. Most turtles can live outside for only part of the year, however, so even if you go with an outdoor pen, you may also need to have an indoor area where the turtle can stay during the colder months.

EXPENSIVE OR INEXPENSIVE PET TURTLES

Turtles do not have to be expensive pets, but owning a turtle can be more expensive than you might expect. In figuring out your turtle-owning budget, you should add the cost of the terrarium and the equipment that comes

with it to the purchase price of the turtle. Terrariums and aquariums can be pricey when you buy them brand new. Depending on the species of turtle and the turtle owner's spending choices, a complete, brand-new setup can cost between $100 and $1,000. However, you may be able to save some money by purchasing a second-hand terrarium or aquarium.

To maintain the healthiest possible turtle, you should research what your species of turtle likes to eat and, more important, what is safe for your species of turtle to eat. For some turtles, simple pellet food and supplements found at the pet store constitute a fine diet. Although this does make a good base diet, most turtles would be grateful for a few

THE TURTLE DOCTOR

Peter Pritchard, PhD—a leading herpetologist—is today's premier authority on turtles. In 1979, he published the *Encyclopedia of Turtles*, which remains one of the most respected books about turtles. Anyone planning to own a turtle should read this comprehensive encyclopedia.

For more than forty years, Dr. Pritchard has worked and lobbied for the conservation of turtles. In 1998, he

established the Chelonian Research Institute in Florida. There, he studies turtles and helps people learn how to preserve and care for turtles. The ten-acre facility contains research laboratories, a library, offices, a residence for visiting scientists, and a museum. The museum has more than 13,000 specimens, including 270 of the 300 species of turtles. This is the world's third largest turtle collection!

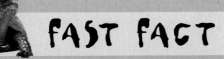

FAST FACT

Herpetology is the branch of zoology that deals with reptiles and amphibians. Veterinarians who specialize in treating reptiles and amphibians are called herpetologists.

fresh vegetables and some fruit every once in a while, so factor fresh produce into your turtle budget.

You do not need any special license to own a pet turtle, and turtles don't require any costly vaccinations. Soon after you purchase your turtle, however, you should take it to a veterinarian or herpetologist to make sure everything is okay. You should not need any costly operations for a standard, healthy turtle.

Turtles do not require expensive annual shots and usually do not need to go to the veterinarian very often as long as they receive proper care. Keep in mind, however, that not all veterinarians treat reptiles and turtles. You may need to drive a distance to find a veterinarian who will accept your pet turtle as a patient. If you do need to take your turtle to a veterinarian, you should be charged only the standard patient fee.

CHAPTER TWO

Types of Turtles

In general, the word *turtle* refers to all reptiles with a shell. All turtles belong to the scientific order Chelonia. Therefore, scientists and veterinarians often refer to turtles, tortoises, and terrapins as "chelonians."

Many people use the word *turtle* to refer to all chelonians. But there are differences between turtles, tor-

toises, and terrapins—in particular, the habitat in which each of these creatures lives. The word turtle refers specifically to chelonians that spend most of their time in the water. These include a large variety of both saltwater and freshwater turtles. The word tortoise typically describes a land-dwelling turtle that almost never enters the water, such as the desert

A sea turtle glides through the ocean water with ease.

tortoise. The final group, terrapins, live near bodies of water, such as ponds, lakes, or marshes, and spend time both on land and in the water. Terrapins often live in a mixture of salt water and freshwater called "brackish water." In the United States, people generally reserve the word terrapin for a specific species of turtle called the diamondback terrapin. These turtles are common in the salt marshes along the coast of the Atlantic Ocean.

CHARACTERISTICS OF ALL TURTLES

Whether people call them turtles, tortoises, or terrapins—or by some other nickname, such as "sliders" or "snappers"—these shelled reptiles all share a few common characteristics, beginning with their ectothermic bodies. *Ectothermic* is a scientific term meaning cold-blooded. This means that an animal relies on heat from outside its body to keep its body temperature at a comfortable level. Snakes, lizards, frogs, salamanders, and turtles are all cold-blooded. A person who passes by any pond on a warm, sunny day will likely notice a number of turtles sunning themselves on fallen logs or rocks. Like people, turtles need heat to activate chemicals in the body that carry out bodily processes. Unlike people, however, turtles cannot produce their own heat. If the tempera-

ture surrounding a turtle drops, the turtle's body temperature will also go down.

All turtles also have a keen sense of smell. Like other reptiles, turtles are equipped with a special organ called the vomeronasal organ (VNO), or the Jacobson's organ. The VNO is located on the roof of the turtle's mouth. The olfactory nerve, which sends messages about smells to the brain, serves as a direct route from the VNO to the brain. When a turtle wants to gather information about a potential mate, feeding spot, or food, it can use its VNO to help it smell—even underwater! A turtle accomplishes this task by opening its mouth, catching odor particles on its tongue, and moving them to its VNO. The VNO then sends a message to the turtle's brain for processing.

In addition to a highly developed sense of smell, turtles also have excellent vision. Turtles' eyes can quickly pick up on movement, which allows them to sense predators or possible snacks from far away. When kept in captivity, some turtles—most tortoises, for example—learn to recognize their owner by sight.

Although turtles have well-developed senses of sight and smell, their sense of hearing is not as good. Unlike people, turtles do not have an outer ear. Turtles do have the middle and inner ear mechanisms, however, which allow them to hear sounds. They can hear low-pitched sounds better than they can hear high-pitched sounds. In addition, turtles can use their legs and shells to sense vibrations in their surrounding environment.

Turtles' shells are quite sensitive. Many people mistakenly believe that a turtle's shell is virtually indestructible. In fact, the opposite is true. A turtle's shell has nerve endings, which means that a turtle can tell when something touches its shell. Turtles can feel pressure and pain through their shells. A turtle's shell is

an important part of its skeleton; the shell is attached to both the spine and the rib cage.

The upper part of a turtle's shell is called the carapace, and the lower part, or underbelly, is called the plastron. A bridge of small bones connects the carapace to the plastron. Both the carapace and the plastron are covered with scutes, which are patches of a material called keratin—the same material that makes up a horse's hooves and a person's hair and fingernails. Between the scutes are thin growth areas that are extremely sensitive. The scutes on both the carapace and the plastron

THE TURTLE'S SHELL

The domed outer part of the turtle's shell is called the carapace, while the hard underbelly is known as the plastron.

sit atop the underlying bony plates and give the shell extra strength and support. The scutes on many turtles' shells create beautiful, colorful patterns, while the scutes on others are dull brown or black.

Another characteristic of all turtles is the rather small area of the brain that controls learning. This does not mean that turtles lack intelligence; it simply means that they are unlikely to learn to do tricks for onlookers. Turtles that live primarily on land, such as tortoises, tend to learn faster than other turtles. Turtles are creatures of habit and can learn to recognize some routines, such as feeding or snack time. You may have heard the old saying that, "The way to a man's heart is through his stomach." The same is true of turtles. Giving a turtle its favorite treat as a reward for accomplishing a certain task—for example, responding when you call its name—will help a turtle to learn. Some turtles can learn to recognize their owners as the source of their food and will follow them around in hopes of earning a tasty morsel. As mentioned earlier, some turtles can recognize their owners on sight, and even distinguish their owners from other people in a group.

The final characteristic shared by all turtles is a horny beak.

Turtles do not have teeth. Instead, they have a beak with a sharp-edged jaw that cuts through plant and animal matter much like a pair of scissors. Turtles use their horny beaks to tear off, crush, and shred bits of food. Their horny beaks never stop growing, so turtles kept in captivity occasionally need to have their beaks filed down because their diets often include softer foods than those found in the wild. Wild turtles eat enough rough materials to wear down their sharp-edged jaws naturally.

While all turtles do share a number of common traits, their differences outweigh their similarities. Some turtles live in fresh water, while others inhabit saltwater. Some turtles enjoy basking in the sun, while others rarely leave the water. Some are carnivorous (meat-eating), while others eat only plants. Some stop growing at a mere three inches (8 cm), while others grow as long as seven feet (2.5 m). Knowing the vast differences

FAST FACT

Many turtles eat using the "gape-and-suck" method. They open their mouths; suck in water, food, and other debris; and expel whatever material they do not want.

between the different types of turtles can help you to identify them. The seven main types of turtles include: pond, marsh, and box turtles; snapping turtles; mud and musk turtles; side-necked turtles; soft-shelled turtles; sea turtles; and tortoises.

POND, MARSH, AND BOX TURTLES

One of the largest groups of turtles is the pond, marsh, and box turtles. These turtles are semi-aquatic, which means that they spend part of their time on land and part of their time in the water. Most of these turtles live in or near bodies of freshwater, including swamps, ponds, rivers, streams, and lakes. Others prefer the brackish waters of coastal marshes.

Perhaps the most easily recognized of the pond, marsh, and box turtles are red-eared sliders. These are among the most popular pet turtles. Red-eared sliders are native to the southeastern United States and do well in warm climates. Adult

The red-eared slider is a very common species of turtle found in the southeastern United States. These small, hardy turtles make excellent pets.

sliders grow to be about five to nine inches (13 to 23 cm) long. Red-eared sliders have dark-colored bodies and shells with yellow and red markings. Their red "ears" are located on their head, just behind their eyes. Red-eared sliders are omnivores—that is, they eat both plants and meat. They dine on fish, crayfish, tadpoles, snails, insects, carrion, and plants. Red-eared sliders enjoy basking in the sun. On warm days, they often climb onto rocks or logs and soak up the sun's rays.

Painted turtles are closely related to the red-eared sliders, but they are not quite as colorful. They have dark green or black carapaces and yellowish plastrons. Their legs are black with red stripes on them, and their heads are black with yellow stripes. Like red-eared sliders, painted turtles spend their time basking in the sun. Baby painted turtles are primarily carnivorous, opting to eat worms, insects, and dead fish first, and plants second. Adults, however, prefer plants to meat. Painted turtles range

FAMOUS RED-EARED SLIDERS

In 1976, the movie *Rocky*, about an unknown Philadelphia boxer named Rocky Balboa, propelled actor Sylvester Stallone to superstardom. *Rocky* was such a hit that it won Academy Awards and spurred five sequels, including the 2006 release *Rocky Balboa*. You may ask what a movie about boxing has to do with turtles. The answer is plenty.

In one scene of the original film, Rocky introduces Adrian, his future wife and a clerk at the local pet shop, to his pet turtles, a pair of red-eared sliders named Cuff and Link. Thirty years later, Cuff and Link made another brief appearance in *Rocky Balboa*. The point of interest, however, is that the same two turtles were used in both movies!

In a story for the *Philadelphia Inquirer*, reporter Michael Klein spoke to Cuff and Link's owners during the production of *Rocky Balboa*. Joseph Marks owned the pet shop that served as Adrian's workplace in *Rocky*. When the movie wrapped in 1975, Marks agreed to keep and care for the red-eared sliders. Marks eventually had to close the pet shop, but his nephew, John Stuart, lives in the former store and continues to care for Cuff and Link. When Stallone returned to Philadelphia to start filming *Rocky Balboa*, Marks ran into him and mentioned the turtles in passing. Shortly thereafter, he received a call, asking if Cuff and Link would be willing to make another appearance in the new film.

A painted turtle is easy to identify by the yellow and black stripes on its head and legs.

in length from five to ten inches (12 to 25.5 cm) long.

Bog turtles, sometimes called boggies, are members of the pond turtle family that are becoming rarer. Boggies are among the world's

smallest turtles, growing to be only three to four inches (8 to 10 cm) long. Boggies have orange splotches on either side of their necks, and they sometimes have a reddish-orange color on their legs, brown or reddish carapaces, and brown or black plastrons. Bog turtles are omnivores. They eat worms, slugs, frogs, snails, insects, berries, and seeds. The destruction of wetlands in the United States has caused a decrease in the population of boggies. At the federal level, bog turtles are listed as threatened; in several

TESTUDO, A DIAMONDBACK TERRAPIN

Diamondback terrapins are semi-aquatic turtles that inhabit brackish coastal marshes along the Atlantic Ocean. College students who attend the University of Maryland also proudly call themselves "Terrapins," or "Terps" for short. The mascot of the University of Maryland is a diamondback terrapin known as Testudo.

Since May 23, 1933, Testudo has proudly appeared on the sidelines of numerous sports competitions to drum up support for the athletes. The exact origin of the mascot's name is unclear,

but the university's Web site reports a number of possibilities. One suggests that his name is derived from the word *Testudines*, which is a scientific classification of turtles. Another says that the name was derived from the Latin word *testudo*. The testudo was a formation in which Roman soldiers used their shields to create a barrier of protection over their heads—just as a turtle shields itself inside its shell. Either way, Testudo has been delighting crowds and encouraging athletes for decades.

states, they have already reached endangered status.

While red-eared sliders, painted turtles, and boggies opt for freshwater ponds and swamps, diamondback terrapins prefer the slightly salty, brackish waters of coastal marshes along the Atlantic Ocean. Diamondbacks spend much of their time in the water, but, like other pond and marsh turtles, they enjoy basking on logs on hot days. Diamondbacks have dark gray, brown, or black carapaces that feature a pattern of diamond-shaped grooves and yellowish or greenish plastrons. Diamondbacks have gray or beige skin, covered with black spots. Female diamondbacks are typically larger than the males are and grow to be about six to nine inches (15 to 23 cm) long. Males grow to be between four and six inches (10 to

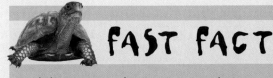

FAST FACT

While some turtles can retract their entire bodies into their shells when they are frightened, sea turtles and snapping turtles cannot because their plastrons are not big enough. This is why sea turtles and snapping turtles have powerful jaws and claws.

15 cm) long. These turtles eat plants and animals, such as snails, crabs, mussels, insects, fish, and water plants. In the nineteenth and twentieth centuries, people considered diamondback terrapin a culinary delicacy. Even though it was expensive, demand for the reptile was high, and hunting nearly destroyed the entire population. Today, laws help protect diamondback terrapins in the wild.

Box turtles are closely related to the pond and marsh turtles, but they often get grouped with the tortoises because they spend a lot of time on land. Box turtles live in a variety of habitats, such as forests, meadows, prairies, plains, and pond and marsh edges. Some box turtles, like Asian box turtles and Gulf

Coast box turtles, spend a lot of time in the water; other box turtles live primarily on land and enter water only if it is a few inches deep. A unique feature of the box turtle is its ability not only to withdraw its head, tail, and legs, but also to pull its plastron upward to completely "box" itself inside its shell. Box turtles from different regions have strikingly different looks. For example, Eastern box turtles have highly domed carapaces, while Western box turtles' carapaces are flatter. Box turtles are omnivores, but they eat more meat when they are young and more plants when they get older.

Other notable members of the pond, marsh, and box turtle family are spotted turtles, wood turtles, map turtles, and sawback turtles. Spotted turtles have spots on their heads and necks. Wood turtles, sometimes called "woodies," are semi-aquatic, but they spend time foraging in woodland areas. Both map turtles and sawback turtles have interesting carapaces. Map turtles' carapaces are covered with intricate markings, while sawback turtles have raised scutes that create a jagged, saw-like appearance.

lakes, and ponds are snapping turtles, which look like leftovers from the time of dinosaurs. The two categories of snapping turtles are common snappers and alligator snappers.

Common snappers have large heads, long necks that can stretch quite far, and strong jaws. These traits—combined with an angry demeanor and a readiness to bite—make snappers a type of turtle that is best to avoid. Common snappers have dark gray, brown, or black carapaces that grow twelve to eighteen inches (30 to 46 cm) long and plastrons that are slightly smaller and lighter in color. Snappers are mostly carnivorous, eating fish, frogs, lizards, small mammals, and birds. They also eat some plants. Snappers occasionally leave the water to bask, but they often warm up by simply floating near the surface of the water. Snappers they

Another type of snapping turtle is the alligator snapper. Alligator snappers have some of the same characteristics as common snappers. They are not quite as aggressive as common snappers, but they are much larger. These turtles grow to be more than twenty-five inches (64 cm) long and weigh more than 150 pounds (68 kg).

Alligator snappers are mostly brown with large heads, strong jaws, and hooked beaks. Their carapaces have raised scutes, which makes them look rough and bumpy. They have long, rough tails. Alligator snappers use an interesting technique to catch food. These turtles lie still with their mouths open. Then they use their tongues, which resemble a worm, to lure in unsuspecting victims. When their prey gets close enough, the turtles snap their powerful jaws shut and savor a tasty meal.

The alligator snapper bears a slight resemblance to its namesake because of its narrow, pointed head, long neck, raised scutes, and bumpy tail. Alligator snappers get very large; up to three feet (almost 1 m) long and 250 pounds (114 kg).

Alligator snappers eat fish, crayfish, worms, insects, frogs, plants, and even other turtles.

MUD AND MUSK TURTLES

Mud and musk turtles share more similarities than differences with each other. Both mud and musk turtles are dull in color, and because they spend the majority of their time in the water, they often develop algae growths on their shells. Mud and musk turtles are rather lazy, but they occasionally leave the water to bask in the sun. Some will actually climb several feet into trees to soak up the sun's rays! Both of these turtles are carnivorous and enjoy foods such as worms, insects, fish, raw meat, and carrion. Mud and musk turtles range in size from the four-inch-long (10-cm-long) American musk turtle to the thirteen-inch-long (33-cm-long) Mexican giant musk turtle. Wild American mud and musk turtles will often try to bite

The white-lipped mud turtle is native to Central America.

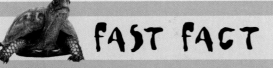

when they are handled. Perhaps the most distinguishing feature of the mud and musk turtles, however, is their ability to secrete a strong, foul odor when they feel threatened. This odor is much stronger in the musk turtles, which has earned them the nickname "Stinkpots."

SIDE-NECKED TURTLES

Another interesting group of turtles is the side-necked turtles. Many turtles can retract their heads straight back into their shells, but side-necked turtles turn their heads to the side and bury them in the space between their necks and their front legs. Side-necked turtles fall into two categories: primitive side-necked turtles and advanced side-necked turtles. Both groups pull their necks to the side, but their bone structures and the arrangement of scutes on their plastrons are different. Both groups are mostly aquatic. Primitive side-necked turtles can be found in

tropical areas like South America and parts of Africa. Advanced side-necked turtles live in South America, Australia, and New Guinea.

Perhaps one of the most easily identified members of the side-necked family—and one of the strangest-looking turtles in the world—is the advanced side-necked turtle called the matamata. The matamata is brown or beige and has a long, broad, flattened neck with a triangular head. Its slender, tube-like nose resembles a pig's snout. It has a rough carapace, which sports a layer of algae that helps camouflage the matamata when it is waiting for food to float past. When matamatas do grab food, they typically swallow it whole because they have very weak jaws. Matamatas are found in several countries throughout South America, especially in slow-moving bodies of water near the Amazon River.

Matamatas are not the only strange-looking members of the side-necked turtle family. Snake-necked turtles have long, slender necks that look like snakes, as their name suggests. Depending on the species, carapaces of snake-necked turtles may be broad or narrow and range in color from gray to black. Unlike matamatas, which are poor swimmers even though they are highly aquatic, snake-necked turtles have strong swimming skills. Snake-necked turtles are native to South America and Australia.

SOFT-SHELLED TURTLES

While matamatas have an oddly porcine head and neck shape, soft-shelled turtles are distinguished by their interesting carapaces. Unlike their hard-shelled relatives, soft-shelled turtles' carapaces are more like flat layers of thickened skin than shells. The carapaces of soft-shelled turtles may be gray, brown, or olive green, with markings in yellow, black, white, and red. The carapaces of some soft-shelled turtles may reach 36 to 48 inches (91 to 122 cm) long, but the North American varieties are usually around 24 inches (61 cm) long. Soft-shelled turtles are built for swimming, with wide feet and

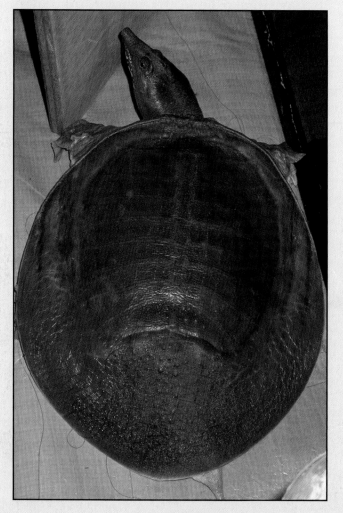

The Chinese soft-shelled turtle, or *Pelodiscus sinensis*, is found in swampy areas of Asia. These aquatic turtles use their long snouts to breathe air while resting in the mud or sand beneath shallow water. The carapace of a soft-shelled turtle is not made up of hard scutes; instead, the shell has the consistency of sturdy leather. Chinese soft-shelled turtles are becoming more popular as pets, although they are best known as the main ingredient in turtle soup! On average, a Chinese soft-shelled turtle can grow to be about one foot (30 cm) long, and it can be expected to live for about 25 years.

webbed toes, but they spend most of their time buried in the sand or mud in shallow areas of lakes, rivers, ponds, and other bodies of water. When buried, they often extend their necks and heads so they can stick their noses above the surface of the water to breathe. Soft carapaces may make these turtles seem more approachable than their hard-shelled counterparts, but do not be fooled! Soft-shelled turtles are carnivores, and they will not hesitate to bite.

SEA TURTLES

The next group of turtles—marine, or sea, turtles—probably gains most of

its recognition from conservation efforts. According to the World Wildlife Fund (WWF), six of the seven species of marine turtles are listed as either endangered or critically endangered. Leatherback sea turtles in the Pacific Ocean, for example, are on the brink of extinction. Among the many threats that sea turtles face are habitat destruction, pollution, and erosion or destruction of nesting beaches.

Sea turtles live primarily in coastal waters and in the wide-open waters of the world's oceans and seas. They have heart-shaped carapaces, which are widest near their

A leatherback sea turtle pushes himself along a beach. These turtles have become endangered because of human development on the beaches where they lay their eggs.

heads. The various species range in size from two to seven feet (0.6 to 2 m) long. They have paddle-shaped limbs, which help to propel them through the water. Most sea turtles feed on mussels, crabs, jellyfish, and fish. Adult green sea turtles, however, are herbivores and feed only on plants.

Leatherback sea turtles are the largest turtles—and one of the largest living reptiles—in the world. These turtles, named for their leathery black shells, can grow to be six and a half to seven feet (about 2 meters) long and weigh more than 1,500 pounds (681 kg). Other species of sea turtles include the green, flatback, loggerhead, Atlantic (or Kemp's) ridley, olive ridley, and hawksbill turtles.

TORTOISES

While sea turtles spend the majority of their time in the water, tortoises live primarily on land, and they rarely—if ever—enter the water. Most tortoises have dome-shaped carapaces and dry, rough skin. The exception is the pancake tortoise, found in certain regions of Africa, which has a rather flat carapace. Many tortoises feed mainly on grass, greens, mushrooms, and other plants. A few species also eat slugs, insects, earthworms, and other ani-

mals. Like other turtles, tortoises grow to be a wide range of different sizes. Some are as small as four inches (10 cm) long, while others, such as the Galápagos giant tortoise, grow more than ten times that size. Tortoises' habitats range from deserts to grasslands to rain forests. Those accustomed to life in dry, sandy areas do poorly when moved to moist, humid environments and vice versa.

Perhaps the most famous members of the tortoise family are the Galápagos giant tortoises. These turtles are native to the Galápagos Islands, which are situated near the equator in the Pacific Ocean. Galápagos giant tortoises are known for their elephantine legs, mammoth carapaces, and slow movement. They feed on plants, such as grasses, leaves, and cacti, which also provide them with most of the water they need to survive. One of the most amazing things about these enormous reptiles is their extremely long life spans. The average life span of a giant tortoise living in the wild is over 150 years!

Other tortoise species are not as large as the giant tortoises; what they lack in size, however, they make up for in beauty. Indian star tortoises and leopard tortoises, for example, have intricate patterns on

The majestic Galápagos giant tortoise is one of the world's largest reptiles.

their carapaces. Noticeable markings on other tortoises include orange or red scales, which are found on the head and limbs of the South American red-footed tortoise, and yellow scales on the South American yellow-footed tortoise.

❧❧❧❧

Due to vast differences in size, habitat, and behavior, as well as strict conservation and protection laws, not all turtles would—or even could—make good pets. Some are too sensitive to changes in the environment, while others are on the verge of extinction. Still others are simply too aggressive. Chapter 3 will help you determine which turtle is best for you.

CHAPTER THREE

Finding the Right Turtle

As with any pet, owning a turtle involves responsibility and commitment. Once you have decided to get a turtle, you need to choose the turtle that is right for you. Not all turtles are ideal for beginners—some turtles are more difficult to care for than others. To decide which turtle is the best fit for you, you have to consider a few factors.

You need to decide what color and size turtle you want to keep, whether you plan to keep the turtle indoors or outdoors, how much space you have to keep the turtle, and how often you would like to interact with your turtle. If you already have turtles and you would like to add more turtles to your collection, you have to determine

Consider your lifestyle when deciding on a turtle, as their needs vary by species.

whether a new turtle will get along with the turtles you already have.

Something else to decide is whether you would rather have a terrestrial species, an aquatic species, or a semi-aquatic species. This decision is important because terrestrial and aquatic species differ significantly from each other. Terrestrial turtles are generally easier to care for and to house, but they are more expensive and they do not tolerate changes in their environments as well as aquatic species do. If you would like to interact with your turtles, however, a terrestrial turtle is a better choice. Aquatic species do not like to be handled—they would rather be observed and left alone. Terrestrial species are much more responsive to their owners and like being handled occasionally.

Typically, turtles have longer life spans than other pets. Some turtles live for twenty to thirty years. Before buying a turtle, you should decide whether you can commit to a pet that might live this long. You must also consider that owning some turtles can be expensive. The best turtles for beginners should be tame, gentle, and easy to handle. You should pick a turtle that will grow only to a medium size as an adult. A good turtle for beginners has a diet that can be easily provided. It can

be difficult as a beginner to maintain precise conditions in a terrarium, so choose a turtle that can live in a range of environments and can tolerate moderate change.

All species have their own requirements, so you will have to learn about whichever specific species you decide on. The best aquatic species for beginners are red-eared sliders, painted turtles, Florida red-bellied turtles, musk turtles, mud turtles, and matamatas. The best terrestrial species for beginners are Asian box turtles, redfoot tortoises, Bell's hingeback tortoises, and Russian tortoises.

Not all turtles are appropriate as pets, especially for beginners. Wild-caught turtles, for example, should never be kept as pets—turtles that are free outside should stay that way. The number of turtle owners has increased, and so has the number of collectors who capture turtles to keep as pets, despite admonitions not to. This, along with environmen-

fAST fACT

The *Guinness Book of World Records* lists a Madagascar radiated tortoise named Tui Malila as the world's oldest known tortoise. He lived to be 188 years old!

tal changes brought on by pollution, has put many species of turtles in danger of extinction. The populations of some species have decreased dramatically.

All turtle owners have a responsibility to seek out and keep captive-bred turtles. Beginning turtle owners should choose widely available, captive-bred species. After gaining some experience, these turtle owners can pick rarer turtles, but turtle owners should always collect captive-bred species. No matter how much experience

FAST FACT

The scientific, Latin names of turtles are often based on the name of the person who discovered the turtle. Sometimes, these Latin names describe something about that type of turtle, such as its color, size, or natural habitat.

you have with turtles, always avoid wild-caught turtles.

To help protect endangered turtle species, turtle owners should never keep as pets North American box

A turtle that is found in the wild should remain in the wild. Never try to domesticate a turtle that you find outdoors.

turtles, such as three-toed box turtles and Gulf Coast box turtles. These species used to be quite common among turtle owners, but many were wild-caught and their environments were destroyed. Now, for these reasons, these turtles are listed as a threatened species by the Convention on the International Trade in Endangered Species of Wild

PROTECTING ENDANGERED SPECIES

The Convention on the International Trade in Endangered Species of Wild Fauna and Flora (CITES) is an agreement between the governments of different countries. This agreement helps ensure that the international trade in animals and plants does not put these specimens in danger of extinction. The international trade in animals, plants, and products such as food, leather goods, and medicines that contain plants and animals is big business.

Until the 1960s, there was no regulation of the trade of endangered plants and animals. International trade, along with environmental factors, had severely decreased the populations of some plants and animals. In 1975, representatives from eighty countries began CITES, which was first drafted in 1963. CITES helps countries make sure that endangered species are not traded.

The CITES list protects over 30,000 species of plants and animals. Today, more than 150 countries voluntarily adhere to the regulations set forth by this international convention. Each country that is a member of CITES passes and enforces its own regulations regarding the trade of endangered species.

The yellow-margined box turtle, or Cuora flavomarginata, is an endangered species that is protected under CITES.

Fauna and Flora (CITES). These types of turtles are almost never captive-bred, so keeping them as pets further decreases the populations of this beautiful species. As a responsible turtle owner, you should avoid keeping these turtles and others that are in danger of extinction, such as the diamondback terrapin.

Snapping turtles—both common snappers and alligator snappers—are also very bad for beginners. Full-grown common snappers can grow to be 18 inches (46 cm) long and weigh up to 40 pounds (18 kg). These turtles are easy to house, but snappers are extremely aggressive. They can inflict serious wounds; they have enough power in their bites to take off a person's fingers. Full-grown alligator snappers can grow to be three feet (91 cm) long and weigh up to 250 pounds (114 kg)! Alligator snappers are capable of inflicting serious wounds, but because they are not nearly as aggressive as common snappers, they are less likely to do so. These turtles are still dangerous, however, and they are extremely difficult to house because of their large size.

Soft-shelled turtles also make terrible pets for beginners. This aquatic species is named for their soft, leathery shells. Their shells do not have the bony plates that other

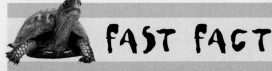

FAST FACT

Some species of aquatic turtles, such as soft-shelled turtles, can breathe through their skin. This allows them to stay underwater for a long time, including during hibernation.

turtles have. Soft-shelled turtles tend to be extremely shy, and when they feel threatened, they become aggressive and bite. They prefer shallow water, and they are sensitive to changes in their environments. Because of their soft shells, they are prone to dangerous shell infections.

BEST TIME TO BUY A TURTLE

The summertime is the best time to buy a species of turtle that normally hibernates. Earlier than May or later than September is a bad time to buy a hibernating species. In the autumn, it is difficult to tell whether an unresponsive turtle is sick or is simply preparing to hibernate. If a turtle is sick before hibernation, it may not survive. The same problem exists in the spring, when the turtle is coming out of hibernation. If the turtle had health problems in the autumn, it may not survive for long after it awakens.

Not all turtles will share their food and living space as nicely as these two. If you decide to purchase more than one turtle, be prepared to separate them in case your turtles do not get along.

Tropical species do not hibernate. You can buy these any time of the year. Remember, however, that tropical turtles are sensitive to cold weather. You might want to wait to buy a tropical species until the weather is warm. Transporting a tropical turtle in cold weather could be problematic, especially if it is exposed to a draft or cold breeze.

This could cause the turtle to develop a respiratory illness, which is potentially fatal.

HOW MANY TURTLES TO GET

By nature, most turtles are solitary creatures. Your turtle is not likely to become lonely, and it does not need a mate. In the wild, turtles sometimes socialize with each other. This is generally done only during mating season. Other times, turtles will socialize for safety reasons—a group of turtles is less vulnerable to predators than a solitary turtle is. Your turtles, however, will not have this problem. If you decide to keep more than one turtle, you need to have two separate terrariums for your turtles in case they do not get along. Turtles that do not get along need to be separated to avoid injuries. If you are planning to breed your turtles, you will need at least one of each sex. This is not recommended for beginners, however, and is best left to turtle owners with more experience.

WHERE TO GET A TURTLE

Pet turtles are available in a number of places. Before you choose to buy a turtle—either from a pet store or a breeder—get at least three references for that place. You may want to ask a local veterinarian, herpetologist, or herpetological society for recommendations.

PET STORES: An easy way to buy a pet turtle is to go to a pet store. When you buy a turtle from a local pet store, you can thoroughly examine the turtle to make sure it is healthy before making your purchase. This chapter will tell you what

to look for when examining a turtle. You may have to look around or request a special order, but you can probably find the species of turtle you are looking for at a pet store.

When choosing a pet store, make sure the store is clean and that staffers take good care of their animals. The people who work in the pet store should be knowledgeable about the animals. They should be able to give you advice about your turtle, and they should be able to recommend a good veterinarian or herpetologist.

VIA MAIL ORDER: Many people choose to purchase turtles through a mail-order dealer. You can use the Internet or ask a local herpetological society to help you locate a commercial breeder or mail-order dealer. This is a good idea because you can choose from a variety of different species. Once you have decided on a species, you can find a mail-order dealer that carries the species you are looking for and ask how much they charge. Always order the species you want using the scientific, Latin name to ensure that you get the same turtle you are expecting.

If you buy your turtle through a mail-order dealer, do not worry about shipping the turtle. Dealers are extremely careful with their turtles, and most dealers ship the turtle in a cloth bag or plastic container. The turtle is surrounded by moist towels or moss to keep it moist and comfortable. This is placed in another container, which is surrounded by newspaper or packing materials. This is then sealed in a box, which helps maintain a constant temperature in the container. The box is marked Live Harmless Reptiles so the delivery company handles the package with care.

If you order a turtle by mail, you should request shipping insurance. This will encourage the delivery company to handle your package with respect and care. You should also specify that a signature must be obtained at delivery. That means you or someone you know will have to sign for the package when it is delivered. This keeps your turtle from being left somewhere you might not notice it, or in direct sunlight, which can increase the temperature inside the turtle's shipping container. When you get your turtle, be gentle while removing it from the packaging. Then give the turtle a few days to adjust to its new surroundings.

TURTLE-BUYING CLUBS: You can also create a turtle-buying club to purchase a turtle. In a turtle-buying club, several people mail-order their turtles at one time to get the order

TURTLE RESCUES

Besides a pet store, another place to get a turtle is from a turtle rescue. There are many turtle rescues throughout the world. These rescues take in abandoned turtles, sick turtles, and turtles that people can no longer care for. When the turtles are in need of care, the rescues have veterinarians and herpetologists who help nurse the turtles back to health. In many cases, this means providing ill turtles with the proper lighting, enough water, and nutritious diets. In other cases, this care may mean fixing shells with plaster casts, administering antibiotic shots, and providing round-the-clock rehabilitation.

Once the turtles are healthy and ready for new homes, people can adopt these rehabilitated pets. You can find many of these rescues on the Internet. For some rescues, you can even complete an adoption application online, or you can print an application from the Web and mail it to the rescue.

shipped together. This reduces shipping costs because the shipping charges will be charged per box, not per turtle. This is much cheaper than ordering turtles individually. To establish a turtle-buying club, call your local herpetological society, or set one up using the Internet.

BREEDERS: Breeders are one of the best ways to get a pet turtle. Local breeders, collectors, or hobbyists who breed a small number of turtles offer a great way for you to obtain a pet turtle. They are often people who began just as you did, and they got to be extremely interested in caring for turtles. This means that they take good care of their turtles, and they are aware that wild-caught turtles should not be adopted.

Breeders have a lot of experience raising and keeping turtles, so they are a good place to get your first turtle. They can answer questions and give helpful advice for getting started as a new turtle owner. Since you'll probably buy from a local breeder, that person may also be able to help when you have questions in the

future. Also, when you buy from a breeder you are likely to get a turtle that is in good health. Breeders would not make money if they did not take good care of their turtles. Breeders generally have competitive prices, similar to those of mail-order dealers, but without high shipping costs.

Breeders, however, are not without their disadvantages. Finding a breeder can be difficult. The local herpetological society can help turtle owners locate breeders. Sometimes

Breeders take pride in raising healthy, happy turtles. Many breeders specialize in a particular type of turtle.

breeders advertise in reptile and turtle magazines, so check out these advertisements. Breeding also takes a lot of money and space, which prompts many breeders to deal with only one species. This can make it difficult to find a breeder who sells the species you are looking for.

WHAT TO AVOID WHEN PURCHASING A TURTLE

When you are choosing a turtle, make sure you are getting a healthy turtle. Getting a healthy turtle can save you money, time, and heartbreak. It is hard to watch a turtle suffer, so you want to make sure you are choosing one without health problems. When you purchase a turtle from a local pet store or breeder, examine the turtle thoroughly.

While you are deciding on a particular turtle, make sure the turtle comes out of its shell. If it does not, you should not buy it. A turtle that will not come out of its shell could be hibernating. If it is not hibernation season, give the turtle some time to come out of its shell. Some turtles are shy and need a little time to get comfortable, so you should always move slowly around the turtle. If the turtle has retreated into its shell and remains there for a long time, however, this could be the sign of a health problem. This can also be a sign that

the turtle was wild-caught or has not adjusted well to being in captivity. Either way, you should not purchase a turtle that behaves like this.

When examining a turtle, you should always lift it up. The turtle should feel heavy. If the turtle feels light, the turtle may be undernourished. Unless you are purchasing a soft-shelled turtle or a pancake tortoise, the shell should be firm and rigid. If the shell gives way to light pressure, the turtle could be undernourished or ill. The turtle's legs should function normally, and they should not be swollen. When you buy a turtle, you should gently pull its legs. If they straighten easily, or if they look limp, the turtle might be undernourished. The skin should appear to fit tightly without folds and creases. If the skin on the turtle's neck and legs has folds and creases, the turtle may be undernourished.

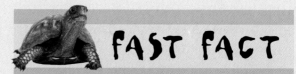

FAST FACT

In 1976, to cut down on the high mortality rates of baby turtles and to prevent salmonella outbreaks, the Food and Drug Administration banned the sale and distribution of turtles with a carapace less than four inches (10 cm) long.

Examine your turtle carefully before purchasing. A turtle that does not come out of his shell may have a health problem.

You do not want to purchase an undernourished turtle—this could mean that the turtle has been poorly cared for, or the turtle could not be eating because of serious health problems. It is very difficult to nurse a sick turtle back to health. When you purchase a turtle, you should bring some fresh greens or produce and try to feed the turtle. You can also ask the person selling the turtle to feed it in front of you. This will show you that the turtle has a robust appetite, which is the sign of a healthy turtle. If the turtle refuses to eat or has not been eating regularly, you should not purchase the turtle.

The turtle needs to be closely examined for pits, cracks, or breaks in its shell. If the turtle has these types of injuries, or if it has missing scutes, it may have experienced some sort of trauma. These problems could have occurred in the wild if the turtle was captured. Missing scutes may be the result of a forest fire, for example. More often, though, damage to the shell occurs when the turtle was raised in unclean, unsuitable conditions in captivity.

Sometimes, an injured shell can heal, leaving only cosmetic scarring. If the turtle has shell breaks or pits that look old and healed, and looks healthy otherwise, it is probably fine to purchase the turtle. Never purchase a turtle if the pits in the shell contain an unclean, odorous, or cheese-like substance, however. This is a sign of severe health problems.

The turtle's eyes should be clear and bright. Check the turtle's eyes while it is out of the water. Its eyes should not have any discharge, and its eyelids should not be swollen. Its eyes should not be crusted. The turtle should follow movement with its eyes.

The turtle should also breathe normally. As the turtle breathes, its nostrils should not bubble, drip, or wheeze. These are signs of a respiratory illness, which can be fatal to a turtle. Open-mouth breathing can indicate an obstruction of the nasal passage. Turtles should always breathe normally through their nostrils with their mouths closed.

You should not purchase a turtle that has unhealed or open wounds

Your turtle's eyes should look bright and healthy, and his nostrils should be clear from any discharge.

on its skin. If the soft parts of the turtle's skin are covered in marks that look like bruises, it may have a fungal infection. Some fungal infections are easily treated, but others may be tougher to get rid of. Fungal infections will look like a layer of cotton or velvet on the outside of the shell. If you are looking at an aquatic turtle and it has a green film on the outside of its shell, it may just have algae growing on it. Algae growths are normal and harmless.

If you plan to purchase an aquatic turtle, you should watch the turtle swim. The turtle should be able to submerge fully into the water without trouble. If the turtle seems to bob up and down or float on the surface as it tries to submerge, this may be the sign of a respiratory illness. The turtle should also swim evenly with both sides as it tries to submerge and swim. If the turtle swims unevenly, this is also a sign of a respiratory problem. You should buy an aquatic turtle only if it can submerge and swim easily and evenly.

Once you have found a turtle that feels heavy, breathes normally, and seems healthy, you may have found the right turtle for you.

CHAPTER FOUR

Giving Your Turtle a Good Life

Turtles that do not get enough of the right stuff—heat, sunshine, and nutrition—are more likely to develop diseases, so you should make sure to set up a proper home for your turtle. Your turtle does not have to live outdoors to get enough heat and sunshine. If you correctly set up your turtle's terrarium, your turtle will have everything it needs.

INDOOR TERRARIUMS FOR TERRESTRIAL TURTLES

Most indoor terrestrial turtles live in terrariums. A terrarium is a small enclosure that mimics outdoor condi-

Three turtles warm themselves under a basking lamp set above their terrarium. Turtles need sunlight and warmth to thrive. If they can't get real sunlight, a basking lamp is the next best thing.

tions. Terrariums can be found at any pet store, or an old fish tank can be transformed into a terrarium.

Your turtle's terrarium should be as large as possible. You may have heard that a turtle will not grow bigger than its enclosure, but this is not true. For the smallest turtles, you can build a terrarium in a fish aquarium—without the water, of course. The terrarium should be at least four times longer and three times wider than your turtle. Your turtle may outgrow the space you have provided, so every few years, you should evaluate your enclosure to make sure it is still the proper size.

A long tank is more important than a tall tank, because your turtle cannot climb the glass sides of a tank. To be safe, the terrarium should be two times taller than the length of the turtle. If you are going to fill your tank with rocks that your turtle can climb, however, you should not provide it with an escape route that will allow it to climb out of the enclosure.

If you are unsure about the height, a lid will keep your turtle inside. A lid will also ensure that other pets, such as cats and dogs, cannot reach your turtle with their paws. Remember that many animals, including cats and dogs, see turtles as possible prey. Even smaller ani-

mals, such as hamsters, may attempt to attack your turtle. Keep this in mind as you set up a home for your turtle. Lids can be purchased at pet stores. Some lids have the two light sources turtles need—simulated natural sunlight and a basking lamp—built right into them.

LIGHT AND TEMPERATURE

If you can allow your turtle to have some natural sunlight every day, your turtle will thank you. Getting sunlight is extremely important to your turtle's health. Without the proper light rays, your turtle will not be able to absorb nutrients into its body.

You do not want to place the tank in direct sunlight, however. You cannot control the heat of the sun, and your turtle could become too warm. It's better to take your turtle out of his terrarium for some sun time each day.

An alternate approach is to purchase lights for the terrarium that

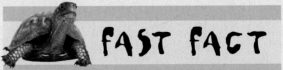

FAST FACT

Many American county fairs hold turtle races. Children set their turtles in a small circle surrounded by a larger circle. The first turtle who crosses the outer circle wins!

simulate natural sunlight. You can visit a pet store and purchase such lights, which are specifically made for reptiles. The bulbs will be labeled "full-spectrum fluorescent light." You should not cover the light source with glass or plastic; this can filter out the light rays that your turtle needs.

Your turtle's lights should be connected to a timer so that you can simulate night and day for your turtle. This transition is important to your turtle's health; the light tells it what to do at a particular time. If your turtle hibernates, for example, the shortening periods of daylight will make it aware that it should begin preparing for hibernation.

Your turtle will also appreciate a nice warm place to bask. An incandescent basking lamp is one of the best ways to provide heat for your turtle. You should place the basking

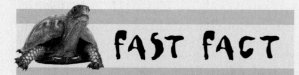

FAST FACT

In 2004, a baby hippo, who was later named Owen, was orphaned near Kenya after a tsunami. Owen was moved to Haller Park Animal Sanctuary, where he met a 130-year-old tortoise named Mzee. Mzee befriended Owen and helped him learn what to eat and how to find safe places to sleep.

lamp out of your turtle's reach. You do not want your turtle to burn itself. Place a flat rock that is larger than your turtle under the light. Many pet stores sell heated rocks for basking, but some veterinarians and herpetologists discourage using these products. They believe that turtles prefer to get their heat from above.

You need to research your turtle's species to determine the proper temperature for its terrarium. Within this habitat, the turtle should have areas that are different temperatures. Your turtle needs a range of about ten degrees Fahrenheit from the warmest area to the coolest. This will enable the turtle to regulate its body temperature by moving to different places in its tank. Place a thermometer in the tank so you can monitor the temperature and make sure it stays in the correct range for your turtle. Stick-on thermometers used in fish tanks also work for turtle terrariums.

Keep your turtle's terrarium away from breezes and drafts, which can cause respiratory illness. Turtles are prone to respiratory illness, and they need to be kept warm for their own health. Also, terrariums should not be close to electrical equipment, which can cause the tank to vibrate. A vibrating tank will be stressful for your turtle.

Since turtles love to hide, give your friend a hiding spot of his own. (Inset) Using astroturf as substrate makes cleaning a breeze because the material can be easily removed, cleaned, and replaced in the terrarium.

FURNISHING THE TERRARIUM

When setting up your terrarium, try to mimic nature. Your turtle will enjoy having rocks or other things to climb and places to hide. Use round, smooth rocks so your turtle will not get injured on sharp edges. Anything you put in your turtle's enclosure should be thoroughly cleaned using a turtle-safe cleaning product. You can put plants in the terrarium, but you should first research the plants to make sure they are safe for your turtle. The turtle might nibble on the leaves, and it might crush them while climbing. Remember that the plants may not continue to look pretty.

The material at the bottom of your turtle's tank is called substrate. You can line your tank with several layers of newspaper or you can create a more natural scene out of dirt and rocks. Pet stores sell several substrates made of various natural materials, such as wood chips or sand. All these substrates need to be cleaned regularly. You should not use regular fish aquarium gravel— turtles might swallow the small pieces and get sick. Aquarium gravel also has jagged edges that could hurt your turtle. You should not use wood shavings as turtle substrate because they have been reported to make turtles sick. A simple strip of Astroturf that fits in the bottom of the terrarium is an acceptable substrate for turtles. Whatever you choose, watch your turtle to make sure it is not eating the substrate. If your turtle does eat the substrate, change it as soon as possible.

Your turtle needs a shallow water bowl in its terrarium. It will drink the water, and it may lounge in its water bowl. Turtles should be able to crawl out of the water and onto land when they need to, so make sure your turtle's water dish is not too deep.

Your turtle also needs a hide box—a small, dark place where the turtle can relax and feel safe. The area should be big enough for the turtle to turn around in, but small enough for the turtle to feel secure.

Once you have come up with a good design for your turtle habitat, stick with it. It is important to design your turtle's habitat and leave it that way. Turtles are creatures of habit. They like to get familiar with their surroundings, so avoid changing the setup of their homes.

THE QUARANTINE TERRARIUM

When you first bring home your turtle, have it spend some time in a quarantine terrarium. The quarantine terrarium allows you to observe your new turtle so it does not contaminate its permanent home or make any other turtles you have sick. Turtles should be kept in quar-

FAST FACT

During the American Revolution, a man named David Bushnell invented the first military submarine. His craft was called the *Turtle* because of its shape. Benjamin Franklin greatly admired the innovation.

antine for a month, so you can see if they show any symptoms of illnesses before housing them in a regular terrarium.

You should give your turtle a bath before putting it in its quarantine terrarium. To do this, place the turtle in a tub of warm water that is shallow enough for the turtle to hold its head above water. After letting your turtle soak for about twenty minutes, you can dry it off with a towel and place it in its quarantine terrarium for the first time.

The quarantine terrarium should be a simple version of the permanent terrarium. The quarantine terrarium should have a water dish, a food dish, and a hiding spot inside. The quarantine terrarium needs to be washed thoroughly with a turtle-safe cleaner every time you use it. Keep the quarantine aquarium for whenever your turtles show any symptoms of illnesses. Chapter 7 will give you an idea of symptoms of illnesses to look for while your turtle is housed in its quarantine terrarium.

INDOOR TANKS FOR AQUATIC TURTLES

When your aquatic turtles live indoors, they live in aquariums much like fish tanks. Aquatic turtles are quite active, so they need lots of room to swim. Their tanks should be as large as possible. Some turtles need only an aquarium with a hiding spot, but most turtles also need an area where they can easily climb out of the water and walk on land. This is called a basking area.

Even turtles that spend most of their time in water need the water to be shallow enough so they can raise their heads and breathe easily. The water should be deep enough, however, that the turtle can be completely submerged. Some turtles, such as painted turtles and red-eared sliders, need much deeper water so they can show off their advanced swimming skills.

Always research your turtle's species to learn how to heat your turtle's swimming area. Some species thrive in room-temperature water, while other species need warmer

Be sure your aquatic turtles have plenty of room to swim. Their aquarium should be large enough to provide a spot where your little friends can climb out of the water and rest or bask in a dry area.

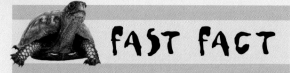

FAST FACT

Sea turtle hatchlings are born with a caruncle, sometimes called an egg tooth. Hatchlings use the caruncle to break through their eggs when they are ready to hatch.

water. To heat the water, you should purchase the same type of heater used in fish tanks. Protect the heater with a cover so your turtle cannot disturb it.

The basking area should be heated with an incandescent basking lamp. This is important for your turtle's hygiene and for maintaining its body temperature. You can use several different materials for a basking area. You could pile up stones or buy a basking area at a pet store. You should make sure any basking area you choose does not have sharp edges. You should also clean all materials with a turtle-safe cleaner before putting them in the tank.

Most aquatic turtles require the same type of lighting as terrestrial turtles: a full-spectrum fluorescent light and an incandescent basking lamp. You also need to filter the water. Filters are extremely important in water-filled turtle tanks. Turtles defecate in their water, so the filter needs to clean the water constantly.

TRACKING SEA TURTLES

The Web site Seaturtle.org tracks over 2,000 turtles as they swim around the U.S. coasts. Seaturtle.org offers tips for scientists, researchers, and turtle lovers about how to tag and track these animals. Scientists attach tracking equipment to the turtle's shell. The equipment sends a message to Seaturtle.org each time the turtle swims to the surface for air. Scientists use this information to design maps of the migration routes of sea turtles and to learn more about the migration habits of sea turtles. The more these scientists know, the better they can protect sea turtles that swim in these areas. They can also use this information to raise awareness about sea turtles.

Before researchers began to use tracking equipment, they tracked turtles using flipper tags. Simple numbered tags were attached to a sea turtle's flipper. When that sea turtle was seen, scientists could identify the turtle from its tag. This process was helpful, but sea turtles spend most of their lives out of sight and underwater. Satellite tracking allows researchers to learn much more about the lives of sea turtles in the water.

You also need to clean the tank frequently. A powerful filter can ensure that your pet turtle has the cleanest water possible, which will keep your turtle healthy. Your water filter should draw in water from the bottom of the tank to ensure that all the water is being cleaned. You should also protect your turtle from the filter's intake valve. If the filter pulls water from the tank too intensely, your turtle could be suctioned next to the valve, leaving it unable to breathe. To prevent this, make sure the intake flow is properly regulated.

OUTDOOR HABITATS FOR TERRESTRIAL TURTLES

An outdoor pen is great for terrestrial turtles, especially if you live in an area where your turtle can stay outside year-round or where it can hibernate outside. Not all turtles can stay outside year-round, however, especially if you live an area with cold winters. Many terrestrial turtles enjoy roaming around the backyard during the summer. Some turtles can stay outdoors from May to September if you have a proper outdoor setup. The rest of the year, your turtles will need to live in an indoor terrarium.

You do not want your turtle to escape, so be very sure you are taking all necessary precautions to keep your turtle safely inside its outdoor pen. You should not leave any spaces that a turtle might be able to sneak through and then get into trouble.

Your turtle's outdoor pen should have high walls that your turtle cannot climb over, with all of the amenities he needs, including a shallow pool in which he can bathe.

Your enclosure's sides need to be high enough so your turtle cannot crawl out into danger. A wire mesh top over the pen will ensure that the turtle cannot escape, and it will deter other animals from attacking your turtle from above.

Your turtle should have some kind of fence around its area. Remember, however, that if your turtle can find a way to escape through a fence, it will. Make sure there is no space between the bottom of the fence and the ground. Even if your turtle cannot squeeze through the space, it still may try. This could cause the turtle to become stuck, or it could damage its shell. Chain-link fences are especially bad for this kind of enclosure. If you have a wooden fence, you should add boards along the bottom if it appears that the turtle might try to crawl through the space between the lowest boards and the ground. The best pens are built of bricks, stones, or wood planks. If you plan to let your turtle hibernate outside, you will have to provide dried leaves, wood chips, or other material in which it can hibernate.

You should remove any hazards that could be potential dangers to turtles. Be sure to research plants that are poisonous to the species of turtle you have. Before placing your turtle in its outdoor pen, make sure none of these plants grows in the area.

Remember that turtles are cold-blooded, or ectothermic. They need sunshine and shade to regulate their body temperatures. You should build rock caves for your turtle to hide in, and make piles of rocks where your turtle can bask in the sunlight. Basking rocks are any flat rocks that are larger than your turtle and outside of water. Your turtle also must have a bathing pot. Try to create a small pond where the turtle can wash, drink, and swim. The water should not be very deep, since terrestrial turtles cannot swim well. This pond will get dirty regularly, so clean the pond often. Be sure to provide a feeding area for your turtle as well.

OUTDOOR PONDS FOR AQUATIC TURTLES

Like terrestrial turtles, aquatic turtles can live outdoors, but this works best if you live in an area that is warm all year round. An outdoor turtle area always needs plenty of areas with direct sunlight and other areas that provide shade. An outdoor area for your aquatic turtles should be generally the same as an area for your terrestrial turtles, but with one major difference. Aquatic turtles require a pond or a swimming area.

PLANTS THAT ARE POISONOUS TO TURTLES

Many common plants are toxic, so turtle owners must be sure to keep their pets away from them. Following is a list of some common plants that present a health hazard to turtles:

Arrowhead Vine	Fiddleleaf Fig	Needlepoint Ivy
Azalea	Foxglove	Nephthytis
Begonia	Gardenia	Nightshade
Bird of Paradise	Grape Ivy	Oleander
Boston Ivy	Heart Ivy	Parlor Ivy
Boxwood	Heavenly Bamboo	Periwinkle
Buttercup family	Holly	Philodendron
Caladium	Hyacinth	Poinsettia
Calla Lily	Ivy	Pothos
Candytuft	Jerusalem Cherry	Pyracanthra
Castor Bean	Juniper	Rhododendron
Chinese Evergreen	Lantana	Rosary Bean
Chinaberry	Lily of the Nile	Rubber Tree
Creeping Charlie	Lily of the Valley	Schefflera
Crowfoot	Lobelia	Shasta Daisy
Cyclamen	Majesty	Spider Mum
Daffodil	Marigold	Split Leaf Philodendron
Dianthus	Mistletoe	String of Pearls
Dumb cane	Morning Glory	Sweet Pea
Elephant's Ear	Mother-in-Law Plant	Umbrella Tree
Euphorbia	Mother-in-Law Tongue	
Ficus Benjamina	Mushrooms	

Source: California Turtle and Tortoise Club

A turtle's pond should be about one and a half feet (46 cm) deep and about ten feet wide. You should line your turtle's pond with protective material. Cover this liner with sand before you fill the pond with water. If you fill your outdoor turtle pond with the correct plants, they will entertain your turtle, and it will feed on them also. You should provide rock ramps and other features to help your turtles get into and out of their ponds. Just like an indoor tank, an outdoor pond needs a filter.

GETTING HELP WITH TURTLE CARE

After you purchase your turtle, you should take it to a veterinarian who is experienced in working with reptiles, or a herpetologist. Even if you think you have chosen a healthy turtle, you should still have a veterinarian check its health. To help the veterinarian determine if your turtle has worms or other infections, bring a stool sample to your turtle's first appointment.

Your local herpetological society will be another good resource when you have questions about your turtle's care. Herpetological societies can be found all over the world. A quick online search will list one for just about every U.S. state. If you have concerns about your turtle, herpetological societies offer a connection to lots of people who are knowledgeable about turtles.

Herpetological societies are dedicated to providing turtle lovers with the most up-to-date information about their pets. Since herpetological societies are usually local, they can provide you with information about turtle species living in your area. Some herpetological societies cater to specific species or certain aspects of turtle culture, so check out a few herpetological societies—not just the one that is closest to you.

Another benefit of getting involved with your local herpetological society is the chance to interact with other turtle owners. You can learn all sorts of things about turtles from fellow members, and you can share stories about turtles with them. Your local herpetological society can also help you find a veterinarian or herpetologist who is qualified to work with your turtle.

When you have questions about your turtle, your best resource is a herpetologist. Look in your phone book or search online for a herpetologist near you.

IF IT WAS NOT MEANT TO BE

If you just cannot keep your turtle anymore, find it a new home in a humane way. You can use the

HAPPY BIRTHDAY, TURTLE!

Unless you know when your turtle was born, you cannot be sure of its exact age. You can make an educated guess, however. One way you can tell is by researching the average size of an adult of your turtle's species. Measure your turtle and see how it compares. Most turtles live for at least twenty years.

Some books say that you can calculate a turtle's age by counting its growth rings, which appear on every scute (right). However, keep in mind that the rings can appear to run together in an older turtle, making them difficult to count accurately. Like all other methods of determining your turtle's age, counting growth rings will only give you a rough estimate.

Internet to locate a rescue that accepts turtles. Many people buy small pet turtles because they are cute and seem fun, and then they become overwhelmed by the amount of care they require. This leaves many turtle shelters overrun. You might not be able to find a rescue that is accepting turtles. Contact your local herpetological society—often, members will be able to help find good homes for orphaned turtles.

You should never release your turtle into the wild. Turtles that are used to being provided with food are unable to find their own food in the wild. Turtles that are accustomed to warm temperatures year-round will get sick on a cold night. Turtles that have been pets are unable to survive on their own. Simply releasing your turtle into the wild is never a good idea.

CHAPTER FIVE

Nutrition, Exercise, and Training

Turtles require a lot of care to stay healthy. A responsible pet owner needs to understand the specific nutritional and physical needs of a turtle. Proper care will guarantee that your cold-blooded friend has a healthy and happy life.

Since there are hundreds of species of turtles, making sure your pet gets the right nutrition is often complicated—but it is not impossible. The first step in understanding the foods that are right for your turtle is researching your turtle's species. Turtles from different regions of the world require different kinds of food. You would never feed a leopard tortoise the same diet as a

Terrestrial turtles just love fresh greens, and may nibble throughout the day.

box turtle. Improper nutrition can cause serious digestive problems that can severely injure or kill a turtle.

Some general rules can help you understand the nutritional needs of your turtle. Feeding a terrestrial turtle is different from feeding an aquatic turtle. Almost all tortoises are herbivores; that is, they eat only plants. Box turtles and species from wetter climates, such as the South American redfoot and yellowfoot tortoises, are exceptions to this rule. These turtles prefer meat in their diets. Aquatic turtles are carnivores; they usually eat small fish, snails, and mollusks. Terrapins are omnivores; they eat both meat and plants. Although these rules are helpful, certain species cannot eat particular foods. Tortoises from arid climates, for example, cannot eat fruits because the high sugar content could bring on diarrhea or dehydration. Understanding your turtle's needs ensures that it will receive the proper nutrition.

FEEDING TERRESTRIAL TURTLES

In the wild, many terrestrial turtles graze as they work their way across a habitat. They eat a wide variety of plants during their travels. Wild tortoises consume grasses, flowers, and leaves. You should always check for any specific foods your turtle's

species might require. Most terrestrial turtles require a diet that is 90 percent vegetable-based. Coarse mixed grasses, cabbage, and clover leaves are good bases for tortoises. They will also enjoy dandelions, carrot tops or peelings, and parsley. Tortoises like eating flowers, but some flowers can be toxic to certain species. Before feeding your tortoise any flowers, do some research. Never give your tortoise any chemically treated plants. The other 10 percent of a terrestrial turtle's diet should consist of fruit. However, the high levels of sugars in fruits can be too rich for some species. It is important to offer fruit only as a special treat and not as a regular part of your turtle's diet. Some fruits that tortoises savor include melons, apples, pineapples, pears, and blueberries.

Though some tortoises come from arid climates, where water is hard to come by, your turtle should have fresh water every day. The bowl

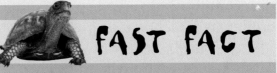

FAST FACT

Do not be surprised if your turtle eats a snail—shell and all. The snail's shell is an excellent source of calcium, and your turtle will thoroughly enjoy this tasty, crunchy treat!

Your turtle may enjoy a fruity treat from time to time, but fruit should not be a part of his daily diet.

should be shallow and should not tip over easily. Terrestrial turtles also enjoy an occasional soak in water, so the bowl should be easy to climb into. It is essential to change the water daily to avoid buildup of harmful bacteria, such as salmonella.

Terrestrial turtles can go for long periods without food, but you should feed your turtle at least once a day. In the wild, tortoises like to graze, so you should try to serve yours several small meals each day. If this does not fit into your daily routine, one meal a day is sufficient. You should never provide your turtle with too much food. Turtles tend to overeat, so overfeeding them can lead to an overweight, unhappy turtle. It is also important to remove any uneaten

food from the habitat before it spoils. Spoiled fruits or vegetables can pose a serious health risk to your turtle. You should remove and throw away food your turtle does not consume at the end of each day.

Supplements are a vital part of every turtle's diet. They stave off vitamin and mineral deficiencies. Terrestrial turtles living in captivity often do not get the same exposure to unfiltered sunlight that they would in the wild. This can cause a vitamin D3 deficiency, which can hamper your turtle's ability to absorb calcium. While calcium is an important mineral for the bone health of all animals, it is especially critical to turtles. A calcium deficiency can lead to softening of the shell and serious health ailments, such as metabolic bone disease (MBD). You can easily avoid this problem by properly supplementing your turtle's diet. Purchase a phosphorous-free calcium powder from a local pet store and add a pinch to every other meal. You can also leave a calcium-rich cuttlebone in the tank for your turtle to nibble on.

Some turtle owners also crush a multivitamin tablet and put it in their turtle's food once a week to prevent vitamin deficiencies. This is controversial among some experts. Some veterinarians and herpetologists argue that a suitable diet will provide a turtle with all the nutrients it needs and that a multivitamin could lead to a toxic buildup of vitamins A and D.

If you are concerned that your turtle is not getting the right amount of minerals, consult a veterinarian or herpetologist before adding a multivitamin to your turtle's diet. Your veterinarian is the best person to assess what your turtle's diet is lacking. Remember that adequate lighting is an important part of your turtle's health and aids in the absorption of necessary vitamins and minerals.

FEEDING AQUATIC TURTLES

Feeding an aquatic turtle can be messy. Unlike their land-loving cousins, aquatic turtles cannot use

PHOSPHOROUS AND CALCIUM

All turtles need phosphorous and calcium for proper growth. In captivity, it is difficult to maintain the proper levels of these two elements. While many of the foods served to captive turtles contain enough phosphorous, many lack the needed calcium. An excess of phosphorous is very dangerous to your pet's health. This is why calcium supplements are necessary for good nutrition.

It is your responsibility as a turtle owner to know the foods that have a poor phosphorous-to-calcium ratio.

Grapes, bananas, mealworms, crickets, and fresh peas should be avoided. Spinach is dangerous to all turtles. The high concentration of oxalic acid in spinach combines with calcium to form an insoluble salt that builds up in the turtle's kidneys. Similar problems can occur with bok choy and kale. Selecting foods with a calcium-to-phosphorous ratio of 1:1 or better is crucial. Some good options include avocadoes, blackberries, broccoli stems, celery, endive, and green beans.

A HARD-TO-PLEASE PET

Turtles are quite stubborn, especially when it comes to their diets. Most turtles have a very keen sense of taste, which makes them picky eaters. Once they find something they really like, they will often refuse to eat other items you offer them. Of course, they do not always enjoy the types of foods that they need most. Catering to your turtle's cravings could do them more harm than good. This is why it is important to keep your turtle's diet as varied as possible.

If you are having trouble getting your turtle to eat the right types of foods, a little sleight-of-hand may help him get back on the right dietary track. Mix small amounts of other nutritious foods in with your turtle's favorite food. Gradually add less of your turtle's favorite food to the dish. Soon your turtle will be eating a wider variety of foods.

their tongues to swallow food; they rely on water to push food into their stomachs. These turtles also use their powerful jaws to tear their food into small pieces that are easy to swallow. This creates quite a mess in your turtle's tank. Leftover pieces of food collect at the bottom, and they quickly breed harmful bacteria. Even the most powerful filter is not strong enough to handle this mess. To avoid this problem, you should get a separate feeding tank. This feeding tank can be smaller than your turtle's usual home, but it needs to have enough space and water for your turtle to submerge itself completely while eating. Once food is introduced, the turtle is free to make as much of a mess as it likes without

sullying its regular surroundings. After your turtle has finished feeding, wash it off with some warm water and return it to its usual tank. Then you can throw away the leftover food and completely clean the feeding tank to get it ready for the next feeding.

Aquatic turtles are mostly carnivorous. Live goldfish and earthworms are healthy diet staples. It is best to stun or kill live fish before introducing them into the tank so your turtle does not have to spend a long time hunting the fish. You can keep fish in the freezer until feeding, but make sure the fish is completely thawed before you give it to your turtle. Commercial trout pellets and turtle food sticks are another good

Squiggly, wiggly earthworms are a favorite food of aquatic turtles. You can dig them out of the ground in your own backyard, or you can get them from a bait shop or pet store.

feeding option if fish and earthworms are not readily available. Like terrestrial turtles, aquatic turtles do well on a varied diet. You can occasionally offer your turtle snails and cuts of lean meat, such as heart or liver, as treats. About 65 to 90 percent of an aquatic turtle's diet should be protein-based, but they also enjoy a snack of vegetables. Aquatic turtles especially like leafy greens, such as romaine lettuce. They also eat clover leaves, dandelions, and grated carrots. You should always research your turtle's species before offering fruits and vegetables to your turtle. Some fruits and vegetables are simply too rich for certain species to digest. You should give your aquatic turtle some vegetables or fruits with every other meal.

Your aquatic turtle gets its drinking water from its tank. This is why you have to make sure the tank's filter is working properly. You should change the water at least once every four weeks. The fresh water needs to be about the same temperature as the water remaining in the tank. This might mean having two heaters.

It can be tricky to know when and how much to feed your aquatic turtle. Terrestrial turtles are able to graze as they like, but you need to schedule daily feeding times for an aquatic turtle. You should always check guidelines for your turtle's species, but over a week, most adult turtles need to consume about twenty goldfish or earthworms. Remember that you should offer leafy vegetables with every other meal. You should offer your turtle treats sparingly to keep your turtle's diet healthy and balanced.

Like terrestrial turtles, aquatic turtles need enough calcium in their diets. Your turtle obtains some of the necessary calcium from the bones of

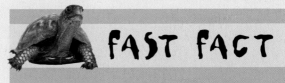

FAST FACT

Leatherback sea turtles are the fastest turtles in the world. They can swim up to 22 miles per hour (35 kmph).

the whole fish it eats as part of its regular diet. Dusting your turtle's food with a phosphorous-free calcium powder is another good option. As with terrestrial turtles, lighting is an important component of an aquatic turtle's well-being. Your turtle's tank needs to offer the right amount of ultraviolet light at all times.

Keep in mind the old saying that variety is the spice of life. This holds true for a healthy turtle as well. Within limits, you should change your turtle's culinary choices and watch it thrive!

EXERCISE

Although turtles seem relatively lazy when compared to other pets, such as dogs and cats, they do require physical stimulation to stay content. Many terrestrial turtles are not good swimmers, so they will not enjoy an outdoor pond. A walk is a much safer option for your terrestrial turtle. You should not allow your turtle to roam freely. When your turtle is out of its terrarium, you should supervise it to ensure that it does not get into trouble. It is fine to clear an indoor space for your turtle to roam, but be sure this space contains no sharp surfaces or small objects. If you have other pets, keep them in another room while your turtle wanders. Once you have closed off an area especially for your turtle, place some food at different ends of the enclosure. Spreading some treats around will entice your turtle to move.

Let your turtles roam free as often as you can, as they will appreciate the exercise. The area in which they play should be free of hazards, and you should stay nearby to keep an eye on them.

If weather permits, you should consider allowing your turtle to roam around an enclosure within your yard. In the wild, terrestrial turtles graze on grass as they walk around. Your turtle might want to do this outside, so be sure your yard is free of plants that can harm your turtle and free of chemicals and pesticides. You should never leave your turtle unattended outside, though. It could easily escape from its enclosure and get injured or become lost.

Turtles can also keep active inside their regular tanks. A small pile of flat rocks is great for both climbing and basking. Turtles feel threatened easily, so you need to provide a place for your turtle to hide, especially if you have other pets. A well-constructed hide box provides your turtle with an important escape. Hiding food under rocks or in the corners of the tanks will also encourage your turtle to keep active.

Although it may seem like aquatic turtles get enough exercise by swimming around their tanks, they also need rocks that they can climb to bask and to head off boredom. It is not a good idea to remove your turtle from its regular tank and stick it in an outdoor pond for a change of scenery. The temperature difference could make your turtle sick. Harmful bacteria in outdoor water could also make your turtle sick. Unless you know you can provide a safe outdoor pool or tank, you should leave your aquatic turtle in its own tank.

Once you establish a setup that your turtle feels comfortable with, you should not change the design. Change makes turtles nervous, so you can introduce new rocks and logs for them to climb, but avoid making any major changes. Turtles are resourceful: They can find ways to entertain themselves and stay active.

TRAINING

Your turtle will never sit or roll over, but turtles can definitely learn. Turtle owners who feed their pets at the same time every day will start to notice that their turtles are ready and waiting for food at feeding time. Turtles can learn how to distinguish their owners from other humans. Some terrestrial turtles even follow

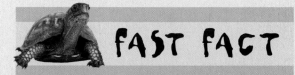

FAST FACT

North American wood turtles are the most intelligent turtles on the planet. Laboratory tests show that these clever creatures can maneuver their way through a maze almost as quickly as rats can.

their owners around the yard like puppies. Some turtles are intelligent enough to learn their own names, but they probably will not come when they are called.

While you will not be playing catch with your turtle anytime soon, you can gain its trust and tame it to your touch. Food is the way to your turtle's heart. You can bring your turtle a piece of its favorite food in a quiet area. Then try to hold onto the food until your turtle gets close and carefully put the food down. Over time, your turtle will associate your hand with a food reward. Depending on your turtle's species, it may eventually take food from your hand. If your turtle is an aggressive species, like a common snapper, however, this is a bad idea.

Once you have gained your turtle's trust, you can work on handling the turtle. Terrestrial turtles do not mind being picked up. They even like to be rubbed on the head, and they

Instruct children to handle your turtle carefully, and always supervise their interaction to avoid any problems.

FAST FACT

When you are trying to tame your turtle, do not wash your hands with perfumed hand soap or hand sanitizer before you handle it. Turtles have a very good sense of smell, so your turtle will recognize you by your scent. Masking your natural odor will confuse your turtle.

may follow you around until you give them the attention they want. Aquatic turtles are far less likely to enjoy any type of handling. You should still handle any turtle from time to time. You will need to handle the turtle during tank cleanings and medical appointments, so your turtle should be used to it. Proper handling will make your turtle less nervous and will keep it from injuring you. The best way to handle a turtle is to pick it up by firmly grasping the sides of its shell. You will have to use both hands to lift larger turtles. Get a good grip on your turtle, so you do not drop it. Finish handling the turtle as quickly as possible. Turtles enjoy having all four feet on the ground, so your turtle will feel more secure once it feels stable again.

Turtles need to be handled gently, so if children will be holding your turtle, you must teach them the right way to pick up the turtle. Turtles are

not like cats or dogs; they should not be touched in the same way as other pets, or cuddled. Children should learn that handling a turtle is done out of necessity, not out of desire to interact with the turtle. You should also limit the amount of time a child handles your turtle to prevent the spreading of disease. Turtles can easily transmit dangerous salmonella bacteria to children. Immediately after handling a turtle, children must thoroughly wash their hands in warm, soapy water. Teach children to enjoy watching your turtle. Explain to them that observing turtles is more entertaining and educational than handling turtles is. Most turtles hide in their shells while people are handling them.

Being a responsible turtle owner begins with understanding your turtle's needs. Turtle owners have the challenge of learning all about their turtle's species. A little time and effort will help you understand how to handle your turtle's nutritional and physical needs.

CHAPTER SIX

Grooming and Hibernation

Turtles do not need much cosmetic grooming. If you keep your turtle and its habitat clean and healthy, you will have few, simple grooming chores. These chores, however, are important to your turtle's health and well-being.

Turtles do not shed all their skin at once, as other reptiles do. They continuously shed their skin in small flakes. Turtles also get dirty, so be sure to treat your turtle to an occasional bath. When you give your turtle a bath, you should always monitor the water temperature. The temperature needs to be the same as the temperature of your turtle's normal habitat. You should not use soap,

Unlike other pets, turtles don't require regular grooming. However, your turtle will get messy sometimes and will need your help to get clean again.

shampoo, or detergent to clean your turtle. Place your turtle in shallow water for a few minutes to soak off any dirt. You can use a soft toothbrush to clean the turtle's shell and claws carefully and gently. You should avoid the growth areas that join the individual scutes. These areas are usually lighter in color and much thinner than the rest of the shell. You should never brush or scratch these growth areas when cleaning your turtle.

CLEANING YOUR TURTLE'S HABITAT

Remember that it will not do much good to clean your turtle's body if you do not clean its habitat. In the wild, turtles have a large area in which to move around; this makes it unlikely that they will choose to live in the same place where they defecate. In captivity, however, turtles must live and defecate in the same terrarium. If your turtle lives in a large, outdoor pen, keeping your turtle's habitat clean will be less of a challenge. Indoor terrariums and tanks, however, do pose a problem. In small habitats, turtles come across their waste more often, and they tend to ingest it while eating. This is why it is so important for you to provide your turtle with a large enough enclosure.

To clean your turtle's habitat, you are going to need to use warm water, paper towels or a sponge, and a turtle-safe cleaner. A turtle-safe cleaner could be a household item such as vinegar or baking soda. These are not safe for all turtles, however. You may need a more expensive, store-bought cleaner specially formulated for reptiles or turtles. You should check with a local pet store and your veterinarian or herpetologist to find a cleaner that is safe for your turtle. Remember that your turtle's species may require a different cleaner than other species of turtles do. Always be sure you are buying something that is safe for your turtle.

For your terrestrial turtle, you should try to provide a substrate that you can clean easily. Newspaper is

Common household cleaners may be poisonous to your turtle. Make sure that chemicals used to clean your turtle's terrarium are turtle-safe.

the substrate that is easiest to clean because you can remove it frequently and replace it with new newspaper. If you use a more natural substrate, such as sand or dirt, it is much harder to clean because the waste will mix with the substrate. These natural substrates will have to be changed frequently to avoid a buildup of harmful bacteria or proliferation of parasites. If you use Astroturf as a substrate, you can remove this and wash it thoroughly with a turtle-safe cleaner.

Every time you clean your turtle's terrarium, wipe down the sides using paper towels and warm water. You may want to add some turtle-safe cleaner to your warm water to make sure you remove any bacteria from your turtle's habitat.

Your aquatic turtle's tank has a filter, and your turtle will eat in the feeding tank. You should still change your turtle's water at least once a month, though. A good time to give your turtle a bath is while you are changing its water. You should wipe down the tank using paper towels and a turtle-

safe cleaner while you are changing the water. You should also check your tank filter's instructions to see how often your filter needs to be cleaned. The instructions will also tell you how to clean the filter.

TRIMMING THE CLAWS AND HORNY BEAK

In addition to keeping your turtle clean, you will also need to trim your turtle's claws and file its horny beak. Just like human nails and hair, a turtle's claws and beak grow continuously throughout its lifetime. Captivity does not provide the same terrain or opportunities for exercise as living in the wild. Therefore, turtles do not have the same occasion to

If your turtle's claws get too long, they will need to be trimmed.

wear down their claws and beaks naturally. If your turtle's diet includes higher-than-normal levels of protein, its claws will grower faster than they would in the wild. If you can, you should allow your terrestrial turtle to roam around on rougher surfaces—such as asphalt or concrete—to wear down its claws naturally. You should also try to monitor protein levels in your turtle's diet.

During your turtle's normal maintenance and grooming, you should check its claws to see whether they are getting too long. You can have your turtle's claws trimmed and its beak filed during its annual veterinarian appointments. You should ask your veterinarian or herpetologist, however, to show you how to trim your turtle's claws so that you do not have to take your turtle to the veterinarian each time its claws get too long. You will need to get special trimmers, which can be purchased at a pet store or on the Internet.

To groom your turtle, you will have to pick it up and position it properly to get a good grip on each foot. You should pick up a small turtle using one hand; gently but firmly hold and lift the turtle at its sides. You can slide your other hand under the turtle's feet so it feels secure. If you have a larger, heavier turtle, however, you will need to use both hands to lift your turtle, being sure to slide your hands as far under the turtle as you can to support it. Turtles like having their feet on the ground, so they might flail their legs while they are off the ground. You should hold the turtle away from your body so you do not get scratched. If you have a side-necked or long-necked turtle, remember that it can reach around and bite you.

To trim the claws, rest your hand on a firm surface and hold the turtle's foot firmly with your thumb and forefinger. Use your other hand to clip each nail at an angle. If you clip too much, you could nick the blood supply and nerve endings, which is painful for your turtle. You should clip just a small amount at a time. Some turtles have translucent claws, so you can see the blood supply, or quick (it looks like a dark line in the claw). Trim the claw to just above the blood supply. If you can't see the blood supply, just proceed carefully and err on the side of caution.

If you do accidentally nick the blood supply, it probably won't cause permanent damage. Keep your turtle dry and clean until the claw stops bleeding, so that the claw doesn't become infected. You can help to stanch the blood flow by putting a little cornstarch on the claw.

Some species of turtles need their horny beaks filed. In the wild, turtles eat grass that contains silica particles, which wears down their horny beaks. Pet turtles are often fed softer plants, and their higher protein diets can cause the beak to grow excessively. Some species of turtles, such as a keeled box turtle, however, use their curved beaks to help them climb. These turtles do not need their beaks filed.

If your turtle's horny beak grows too long, you can ask the veterinarian or herpetologist to file the beak down to its normal length. Or, you can take care of this yourself at home. Hold your turtle on a towel in your lap, and grasp the sides of the turtle's head gently but firmly. You may need to coax your turtle into sticking his neck out of the shell with some food, or just wait a few minutes. Rasp an emery board against the outside of the turtle's beak, until it is reduced to the proper length. It may take several tries to accomplish this, or you might want to spread the grooming out over several days.

CHECKING FOR TICKS

During your turtle's grooming, you should also check its body for ticks. Turtles that are kept outdoors are the most likely to get ticks. Even if you keep your turtle indoors all year round, however, it is possible for it to get ticks. Any soil or plant matter brought in from outdoors can have ticks. People and other pets can also bring ticks in from outside. You can most often find a tick in the folds of skin on your turtle's neck and legs. If you do find a tick there, carefully pull it out using a special tool called a tick puller or using tweezers. You can also use tweezers to remove splinters and loose pieces of shed skin from your turtle.

THE PRICE OF POOR HYGIENE

Both the turtle and its owner can develop serious health issues when conditions are not hygienic. Salmonella is the illness most often associated with turtles. Although it is rare, salmonella infection is a big concern. In the wild, accumulating salmonella bacteria does not pose a problem. In captivity, however, keeping turtles in a constricted environment allows the bacteria to multiply quickly. Keeping your turtle's habitat clean is essential. You should remove

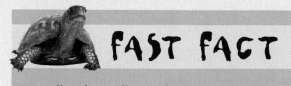

FAST FACT

It is illegal to sell a turtle in the United States without certification that it is salmonella-free.

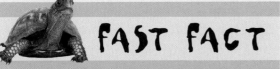

FAST FACT

If the color of your turtle's shell fades or becomes dull as the turtle ages, you can apply a small amount of hoof oil or petroleum jelly and rub it gently into the shell to brighten the shell's appearance. If the application is too heavy, however, the horny layer will not be able to breathe, leading to health problems, and the sticky surface will accumulate dust and dirt.

your turtle's waste promptly and give your turtle fresh drinking water daily. You have to clean your turtle frequently. If you have an aquatic turtle, using a filtration system that includes charcoal will eliminate waste. Feed your aquatic turtle using a separate feeding tank, and clean your filter as often as necessary.

Every time you handle your turtle or any part of its habitat, wash your hands thoroughly, using warm, soapy water. You should always supervise children around your turtle. Watch children closely to make sure they do not put their fingers—or even the turtle—in their mouths when handling the turtle. Immediately after handling a turtle, children should thoroughly wash their hands, using warm, soapy water.

Aquatic turtles occasionally become covered with algae growth,

which is harmless to turtles. You can reduce algae growth naturally, but you should not use chemicals to kill algae. You can use a dimmer light or shorten the time the light is on in the tank to reduce algae growth. Changing the water regularly will also keep algae growth to a minimum. Some turtles use algae growth for camouflage, so you might not want to compromise the delicate balance of the tank. Research your turtle's species to learn what level of algae is healthy.

If your aquatic turtle forms white clumps of material on its skin or

Algae is growing on the head of this wild snapping turtle. This is normal for snappers, as the algae helps them stay camouflaged. For other types of turtles, however, algae growth can be a health concern.

shell, it may have a fungal infection. Fungal infections often begin at injury sites. Fungal infections are serious and can even be fatal if they spread to tissue under the shell, but they are treatable with a simple iodine bath. You can purchase an iodine solution that is right for your turtle at your local pet store. Soak the affected turtle in the iodine bath for ten minutes twice a day until the infection is cleared. While treating a turtle with a fungal infection, keep it in a slightly warmer, dry environment and out of aquarium water. If you ensure that your turtle has adequate dry land to use when it is not in the water—say, large piles of flat rocks— it will be less likely to get a fungal infection.

WHY DO TURTLES HIBERNATE?

Hibernation is a commonly misunderstood part of turtle care. When you are researching your turtle's species, however, you should research whether it hibernates and how and when you should prepare it to hibernate. Some turtle owners "winter" their turtles for up to six months, but captive turtles require only ten to twenty weeks of downtime.

In the wild, hibernation is a dangerous time for turtles. Hibernating turtles are defenseless against predators. Sick, injured, or underweight turtles are vulnerable while hibernating. In captivity, turtles have a much easier time during hibernation, but only if their owners prepare and protect them for the big sleep. Hibernation needs to be carefully controlled. Both in the wild and in captivity, more turtles die during hibernation than at any other period in their lives—specifically at the beginning and end of hibernation.

Most species of turtles that are kept as pets normally have a period of inactivity. Just like your turtle's habitat and diet, hibernation should resemble the conditions a turtle would experience in nature. You will need to research your turtle's species and create hibernation conditions as close to nature as possible. Hibernation is specific to each species.

Turtles native to North America and Europe, such as box turtles, have a period of inactivity during the winter. Loss of food supply and cold temperatures trigger turtles to rest and conserve vital energy. During hibernation, their respiration and heart rates slow. They do not eat or expend energy on digestion. Their metabolism slows, which allows them to survive during cold winter months. It also benefits their reproduction. This type of hibernation is called brumation. Turtles native to very hot climates do not hibernate in the winter. These turtles have periods of inactivity during the hottest season to conserve energy as well. This type of hibernation is called estivation.

AGE, WEIGHT, AND HEALTH CONSIDERATIONS

Before hibernation, you must consider a captive turtle's age, weight, and health. Younger turtles have shorter hibernation periods. You should keep malnourished or sick turtles active during hibernation time. Some turtles should be awakened during hibernation so they can eat. A malnourished or sick turtle will not survive hibernation.

When you are preparing your turtle to hibernate, you should check it for infection. Certain infections cause swelling and inflammation around the eyes or discharge from the eyes or nose. Other common illnesses include necrotic stomatitis, or mouth-rot, which is a highly contagious disorder found in turtles' mouths. Smelly discharge from the tail is a sign of an internal infection. You should also check your turtle for external problems, such as abscesses or sores on its legs, or swelling, lumps, or bumps. A veterinarian or herpetologist needs to treat infections and injuries before your turtle can hibernate safely.

A turtle must store up nutrients and water to survive hibernation. Turtles need to store enough fat to burn during hibernation. Turtles draw energy from stored fat throughout

HIBERNATING OLDER TURTLES FOR THE FIRST TIME

Even if you purchase an older turtle, it is possible that your new pet has not hibernated in the past. If this is the case, you should still prepare the turtle to hibernate using the same steps you would follow for any other turtle of its species. The turtle should settle into hibernation within two or three weeks.

If you have a turtle that does not begin to hibernate after several weeks,

take it out and weigh it. If your turtle has lost 10 percent of its body weight and still has not started to hibernate, it is probably not a good candidate for hibernation. You should take it to the veterinarian or herpetologist immediately for a thorough checkup.

hibernation. If fat reserves are used up too quickly, the turtle's body will break down muscle tissue to survive. Breaking down muscle and organ tissue is, of course, a last resort, and if this continues, the turtle will surely die. If a turtle is underweight at the end of the summer, it will not gain weight before hibernation, and it will lose weight during hibernation.

SEASONAL TRIGGERS

As the temperature drops and the hours of daylight grow shorter, a turtle's instinct to hibernate kicks in. Turtle owners, however, should begin to prepare for the onset of hibernation in late summer—about the middle of August. August might seem early to consider hibernation, but under natural conditions, turtles begin to reduce their food intake four to six weeks before starting the hibernation process. Your turtle might slow its movement and eating. It might also bury itself in the leaves.

Some species of turtles are determined to hibernate regardless of temperature or the duration of sunlight. It is unhealthy—even deadly—to keep the temperature up and artificial daylight prolonged when a turtle is preparing for hibernation. If your turtle is healthy and it suddenly stops eating and becomes inactive, you should prepare a suitable

hibernation environment. If you keep your turtle's tank unseasonably warm while the turtle is not eating, your turtle's body is forced to maintain its metabolism without the caloric intake it needs to stay healthy.

WITHHOLDING FOOD

When it is time for your turtle to start the hibernation process, and when you know your turtle is healthy, you should begin to withhold its food. It takes several weeks for food to clear a turtle's intestinal tract, and turtles that begin hibernation with food in their gastrointestinal systems are likely to sustain long-term problems or die during hibernation. When a turtle hibernates with food still in its gastrointestinal tract, the decaying food produces gas that presses the stomach and intestines against the lungs. This causes oxygen deprivation and can suffocate your turtle.

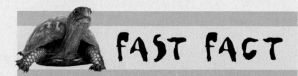

FAST FACT

Brumation is the term used for the hibernation-like state that turtles enter during very cold weather. During periods of extremely high temperatures, estivation provides a way for turtles to "power down."

Turtles need about three full weeks to digest all food and defecate prior to hibernation. Eliminate all feedings, but continue to provide fresh water daily. Bathing your turtle in warm water several days in a row will help it move food through the gastrointestinal tract.

BEGINNING THE HIBERNATION PROCESS

As hibernation begins, turn down heat lamps by several degrees each day over several days. Then turn off the heat lamps and warming devices in the turtle's habitat so the temperature is about 50° Fahrenheit (10° Celsius). In two or three days, your turtle's movements should become sluggish. At this point, you can move the turtle to its hibernation box. Before you place your turtle in its hibernation box, weigh the turtle and record its weight to check during hibernation.

A HIBERNATION BOX

A hibernation box provides a safe and comfortable environment for an indoor hibernation. You can make this box by nailing wooden boards loosely together to form a box that is big enough for your turtle. You should arrange the boards so air can circulate easily through the box, but you should put the boards close

An eastern box turtle sleeps snugly inside his hibernation box, which has been lined with leaves and straw to help keep him warm.

enough to keep the turtle in and predators out. A plastic container will also work, if you drill air holes into the top and sides.

Place pumice or lava rock in the bottom of the hibernation box. Then place moist garden soil over the rocky layer. Over the soil, add peat moss and leaves. After placing your turtle in the hibernation box, cover the box with a fine mesh or cheesecloth. The hibernation box can be placed in a cool basement with a consistent temperature of between 32° and 54° F (0 and 12° C).

You should monitor the temperature inside the hibernation area. You can do this by inserting a digital thermometer into the burrowing material or by taping a thermometer to your turtle's shell. Wireless digital thermometers can be a handy device to monitor the temperature remotely.

HIBERNATING OUTDOORS

If you have created an outdoor enclosure for your turtle, be sure it has leaves and loose dirt for your turtle to burrow into. Your turtle needs to burrow down several feet (a meter or so) to stay below the frost line. Your responsibility as a turtle owner is to ensure that the area is secure on the sides, top, and bottom to protect your hibernating turtle from predators.

HIBERNATING AQUATIC TURTLES

An aquatic turtle kept in an indoor tank will begin hibernation when you reduce the water temperature to below 45° F (7° C). Your aquatic turtle will gradually move to the bottom of the tank. It will remain there during hibernation by exchanging oxygen and carbon dioxide with the water. An aquatic turtle that lives outdoors year-round will go into and out of hibernation without assistance, assuming it has been provided with an adequate environment for its species.

MONITORING HIBERNATION

Every four to six weeks during hibernation, you should check your turtle's weight. This activity is perfectly safe and will not wake the turtle or cause it any stress. It is normal for an adult turtle to lose 10 percent of its body weight during hibernation. If an adult turtle loses more than 10 percent while in hibernation, or if a

FAST FACT

In the wild, fire ants and rodents are a threat to hibernating turtles. If your turtle hibernates outside, you should make sure these predators cannot get near your pet.

Two views of an outdoor hibernation pit. The pit consists of a hole lined with plywood (left) to ensure that the turtle will not be buried beneath the earthen material that will cover him during his hibernation. (Bottom) The turtle's head peeks out of the hibernation pit, which has been filled in with straw, leaves and earth.

young turtle loses more than 15 percent, remove it and have a veterinarian or herpetologist check your pet.

While checking your turtle's weight, check the soil and leaf material in the hibernation box. The substrate and leaves might become dry over time. If necessary, add water to the box, making sure that the water drains down through the leaves and into the soil. You should not leave overly wet areas at the top of the box. Some species of turtles need more hydration than others do. Be sure you understand the environment most suitable for your turtle's species. Be especially careful to watch the moisture levels when caring for young turtles during hibernation. Young turtles are more

vulnerable to dehydration than their older counterparts. Some turtle experts recommend offering water a few times during hibernation. Turtles often drink water and go back into hibernation without ill effects.

If you see your hibernating turtle has urinated, do not put it back in the hibernation box. Place it in a slightly warmer environment and begin offering water immediately. This will help keep your turtle from becoming dehydrated. If this happens, you should immediately begin rehydration, and over-winter for the remaining hibernation period. This seems to happen more often toward the end of the hibernation period, so you should check on your turtle more frequently during the last several weeks of hibernation.

COMING OUT OF HIBERNATION

After ten to twenty weeks, depending on your turtle's species, the turtle might start rustling around inside the hibernation box, or you might end its hibernation. If you have kept the turtle in a hibernation box, take the turtle out of the hibernation box and place it in your quarantine tank. Keep the temperature of the aquarium between 68° and 72° F (20° and 22° C); the basking area, if lit with an incandescent lamp, will naturally be warmer. It should not be long

before your turtle is awake and moving about on its own.

REHYDRATION IS CRUCIAL

As soon as it awakens, your turtle must begin to drink fresh water. During hibernation a turtle's kidneys retain urine filled with toxins, and this needs to be flushed out as soon as possible. This is much easier to do by following simple instructions.

Rather than simply putting a dish of water out for the turtle to drink, prepare a bath using warm water that is 75° to 79° F (24° to 26° C). Some turtle experts recommend that two tablespoons (30 ml) of salt should be

When your turtle emerges from hibernation, immediately provide him with plenty of fresh water to drink. Your pet needs to drink in order to flush out all of the toxins that have built up in his system while he was dormant.

added for every quart (0.95 l) of water. Let the turtle bathe for ten to twenty minutes in just an inch (2.5 cm) or so of water (less if the turtle is very small). You will find that the turtle will drink much more freely this way than from a small dish. You can let it drink as much as it wants.

RETURNING YOUR TURTLE TO ITS YEARLY HABITAT

Prepare the turtle's normal living space with the proper temperature and level of light. Offer fresh food and water each day. Along with

becoming rehydrated, the turtle should begin to eat within one week.

EARLY RISERS

If your turtle is awake and actively moving about when you check on it during hibernation, remove it from the hibernation box and weigh it. If it has lost too much weight, have a veterinarian or herpetologist check it for illness. If it has lost less than 10 percent of its body weight, move it to the quarantine tank, bathe it, and feed it as though it had come out of hibernation at the expected time.

CHAPTER SEVEN

Common Turtle Health Issues

All turtle owners want to make sure their pets are healthy and happy. Even if you are extremely attentive to your turtle's housing, nutritional, and physical needs, your turtle can still develop health problems. It is critical for you to recognize serious medical issues and quickly get your turtle to a vet-erinarian or herpetologist. With proper care and attention, your turtle will need only annual checkups at the veterinarian's office.

FINDING A VETERINARIAN OR HERPETOLOGIST

It can be especially difficult to find a veterinarian who specializes in

The veterinarian will measure your turtle's carapace to make sure he's growing properly.

caring for reptiles. Few veterinarians are trained to deal with the specific health concerns that turtle owners face, so finding a qualified veterinarian or herpetologist is not as simple as looking through the yellow pages or getting a recommendation from your neighbor. One of the best ways to find a veterinarian is to contact your local herpetological society. These groups are great resources for turtle owners. You can ask members whom they take their pets to and if they would recommend their veterinarian or herpetologist.

If there is no herpetological society in your area, you can locate a nearby veterinarian—one who treats turtles, that is—in other ways. Contact local breeders and pet shops to see which veterinarians they rely on for treatment. You might also consider calling neighboring universities, wildlife rescue organizations, and local humane societies. You can use the Internet to search several Web sites that list veterinarians by state.

QUESTIONS TO ASK YOUR VETERINARIAN

If you are lucky enough to find a veterinarian who works with turtles within close proximity to your home, asking these questions can help you determine if this veterinarian is right for you and your turtle:

- ✔ How many veterinarians who care for turtles work at your practice?
- ✔ Are you a member of the American Animal Hospital Association (AAHA)?
- ✔ Are you a member of the Association of Reptilian and Amphibian Veterinarians (ARAV)?

- ✔ Did you take a reptile medicine course as part of your training?
- ✔ Do you have any other formal training with reptiles?
- ✔ Do you subscribe to the *Journal of Small Exotic Animal Medicine?*

While finding a qualified veterinarian or herpetologist can be difficult and frustrating, you should not simply go to the first one you find. These veterinarians are few and far between, but this does not mean you should take your turtle to a veterinarian you are uncomfortable with or who you think is not qualified to treat your turtle. Choosing a reliable, well-trained veterinarian is important to your turtle's health.

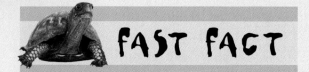

FAST FACT

It is difficult to find a veterinarian trained to treat turtles, but you can start your search for one from your own home. The Internet can help you find a qualified veterinarian or herpetologist in your area.

Unfortunately, your detective work may not pay off the way you want it to. The closest veterinarian who cares for turtles could be far away from your home. This is frustrating to many turtle owners, and it is impractical if your turtle has a health emergency. You may want to consider taking your turtle to a veterinarian or herpetologist outside your area for annual visits and visiting a closer veterinarian in case of an emergency. You should provide your local veterinarian with the contact information for the veterinarian who cares for turtles in case the problem is something your local veterinarian is unprepared to deal with. The veterinarian who cares for turtles should be able to talk the local veterinarian through any immediate problems and stabilize the animal until the specialist can see it. To do this, you will have to get in touch with both veterinarians long before your turtle experiences any health problems.

TREATING COMMON TURTLE HEALTH PROBLEMS

Your turtle may experience some health problems that can be resolved at home by a change in diet or first aid. Certain ailments, however, require the care of a trained professional. Part of your responsibility as a pet owner is to learn to recognize a problem and to seek the appropriate medical care.

DIARRHEA

Diarrhea is a common ailment among turtles. Improper diet, various infections, or worms are the usual causes of diarrhea. If there is no blood in your turtle's stool, you can try ruling out a dietary concern first. Adjust your turtle's diet by removing all fruits. Try offering your turtle dry foods, such as hay and leaves. If the problem persists after several days, it is time to take your pet to the veterinarian. Bring a recent stool sample with you for the veterinarian to analyze.

CHANGES IN URINE

Your turtle's urine should be clear with little white flecks. These flecks are crystallized uric acid. If you notice that your pet's urine has become thick, or if you see an increase in the amount of uric acid, your animal has a health problem. Your turtle might not be getting enough water, which will cause the urine to become more concentrated as the turtle tries to salvage as much water as it can inside the body. You can prevent this by allowing your turtle to soak several times each week. If the problem already exists, however, you should take your turtle to the veterinarian immediately. If left untreated, the turtle's health could quickly deteriorate.

WOUNDS

You can use a little antibiotic cream to treat superficial wounds to the turtle's shell or body at home. These injuries usually result from an accident. Only a trained veterinarian, however, has the knowledge to deal with a deep wound or a badly damaged shell. Your turtle's veterinarian will take the necessary steps to prevent possible infection.

PROLEPSES

Prolepses occur when the lining of the cloaca—a cavity at the end of the urinary and intestinal tracts—protrudes from the anal opening. Internal organs such as the small intestine may be exposed outside the body. This medical issue requires urgent care. If you own a terrestrial turtle, make sure you keep the protruding organs moist until you get to the veterinarian. Any tissue that dries out will die, and your turtle will require surgery to remove it. It is important to keep your turtle from touching the protrusion. Your turtle might not be able to recognize that this is a part of its own body and may try to remove what it considers a foreign object. Restrain your turtle and get it to the veterinarian as soon as possible. The causes of prolepses are unknown, but some experts believe that stress and intestinal worms contribute to the problem.

GOUT

Gout is a serious, but entirely preventable, condition. An excess of fatty foods in your turtle's diet can

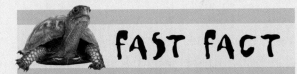

FAST FACT

Because even a slight chill can make your turtle sick, transporting a turtle to the veterinarian in cold weather is a challenge. Keep your turtle warm by placing him in a cotton or linen sack, putting the sack in a cardboard box on top of a hot water bottle, and closing the box. Then cover the box with a blanket, and do not forget to warm your car before taking your turtle outside.

cause gout, especially in terrestrial turtles. This is why it is important to thoroughly understand your turtle's nutritional needs. Terrestrial turtles tend to be herbivorous, so feeding them meat products can adversely affect their health. These turtles' bodies cannot digest fatty foods properly. When they consume too much of this food, uric acid crystals build up in their kidneys and other internal organs. The organs become rock hard and stop working. The best way to prevent this is to know which foods are right for your turtle's species and to keep its diet as varied as possible within the possible dietary parameters.

OBESITY

Obesity is one of the most common problems among turtles in captivity, and it can seriously endanger their health. Excess feeding and lack of exercise are the usual causes of this condition. Improper diet is another contributing factor. You should always try to prevent obesity by feeding your turtle a varied, nutritious diet. Even if your turtle seems to prefer one food to another, offering your turtle many healthy choices is the best way to prevent obesity. If you notice that your turtle has put on too much weight, you can correct the problem by cutting down on fatty, sugary foods.

FAST FACT

Try hiding your turtle's food in different parts of its home. This will encourage your turtle to move around to find its food and help prevent it from becoming obese.

Offer less food at each feeding and scale back on the number of feedings per week. If the problem persists, your turtle may have a serious underlying health problem. You should have a veterinarian examine your turtle immediately.

PARASITES

Although parasites are relatively uncommon in captive-bred turtles, they can be a problem for your pet. If you have an aquatic turtle that lives outside, watch out for leeches. A leech looks like a small, dark worm attached to your turtle's skin; these external parasites survive by

Leeches like this can weaken your pet turtle's health and infect him with disease.

drinking their host's blood. You can remove a leech using tweezers. Then you should apply antibiotic cream to the area. Keep your aquatic turtle out of the water for twenty-four hours to allow the medicine to soak into its skin.

Liver flukes are another common health concern. Infested snails usually transmit these parasites to turtles. Symptoms of infestation include loss of appetite and rapid weight loss. Liver flukes are easy to take care of with a simple trip to your veterinarian, but if they are left untreated, the parasites can destroy your turtle's internal organs.

If your turtle is eating a lot but not gaining any weight, it probably has intestinal worms. Intestinal worms are more common in wild-caught turtles, but captive-bred turtles can also contract intestinal parasites through contaminated foods. Intestinal worms can rob your pet of vital nutrients, so you will have to take your turtle, together with a stool sample, to the veterinarian as soon as possible. Your veterinarian will usually prescribe deworming medicine to give to your turtle.

INTESTINAL INFECTIONS

If your turtle's waste has become smelly, slimy, and runny, the turtle probably has an intestinal infection.

A protozoan buildup in your turtle's intestinal lining can cause this kind of infection. Salmonella is another possibility. These bacteria easily build up in the water supply of an improperly maintained tank. Only your veterinarian can determine what caused the infection and the best possible treatment to get your turtle back on track.

BREATHING PROBLEMS

Your turtle might have a respiratory problem if it is breathing with an open mouth, wheezing, or snoring, or if it has discharge running from its eyes, nose, or mouth. The first step to take if you think your turtle has a respiratory problem is to make sure it is warm enough. Even brief exposure to a draft can have a severe, adverse impact on a turtle's health. Once you are sure the tank is warm enough, quickly get your turtle to the veterinarian. Respiratory infections can easily turn into pneumonia in many turtles. Your veterinarian or herpetologist may prescribe antibiotic injections. Depending on the severity of the infection, these injections may need to be administered for up to three weeks.

SWOLLEN EYES

If your turtle develops swelling of the eyelids, several problems might be brewing. Insufficient humidity, drafts, improper diet, and injuries are all possible causes. Your turtle could also have an acute vitamin A deficiency. Only a veterinarian can determine the source of the problem. If your turtle's veterinarian determines that your turtle has a vitamin A deficiency, she may recommend supplements and a change in diet. The veterinarian may also prescribe topical or systemic antibiotics.

INJURED SHELL

Shell breaks or injuries are often caused by accidents. Depending on the extent of the injury, you may be able to treat your turtle at home with an antibiotic cream. Serious damage to the shell, however, requires an immediate visit to the veterinarian. Bacteria can easily take hold at the site of the injury, causing ulcerative shell disease or shell rot. This disease is extremely contagious and can spread quickly. While your pet is recovering, you have to sterilize your turtle's tank completely. This helps prevent the disease from recurring and gives your pet the best possible chance to heal.

SKIN PATCHES

Simple fungal infections are usually the cause of fuzzy white or gray patches on your turtle's shell. Poor

FAST FACT

Salmonella, which turtles naturally harbor on their skin, is just as dangerous to humans as it is to turtles. Always wash your hands with soap and warm water after handling your turtle, and clean and change your turtle's water regularly to prevent buildup of the bacteria.

water quality contributes to this condition. Adding the fungicide acriflavin, which you can find at a pet store, to your turtle's water can help solve the problem. Monitor your turtle's condition; if the patches do not begin clearing up, make an appointment with your veterinarian.

OVERGROWN BEAKS AND CLAWS

In the wild, a natural diet and the rugged terrain regularly wear down a turtle's beak and claws. In captivity, turtles often have little opportunity to wander outdoors, so their claws continue to grow. A soft diet will not naturally file down a turtle's beak. Too much protein in your turtle's diet will cause the beak and claws to grow excessively. An overgrown beak or claws can keep your turtle from eating and moving around. Information about trimming your turtle's beak and claws is discussed in Chapter 6.

Keep an eye on your turtle's beak to make sure it does not become overgrown.

MINERAL DEFICIENCY

Improper diet is the usual cause of mineral deficiency. If your pet is experiencing this problem, you might notice it eating large quantities of sand or gravel. A blockage of the gastrointestinal tract can occur if your turtle ingests too much of these materials. Add a vitamin supplement

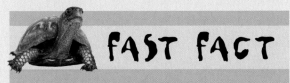

FAST FACT

Foods like tomatoes, bananas, and peaches are high in phosphorous, and too much phosphorous in your turtle's diet can lead to health problems. You should avoid feeding your pet these high-phosphorous foods. If you do offer them, balance the meal with a calcium-rich food like broccoli stems.

to your turtle's food and consider adjusting its diet. If the behavior continues, see your veterinarian to determine what is best for your turtle.

CALCIUM DEFICIENCY

Calcium is essential to shell and bone growth, but it is often difficult for turtles in captivity to get the necessary amount of calcium through the foods they eat. Young aquatic turtles are especially susceptible to calcium deficiencies. Calcium deficiencies are characterized by the shell softening and by malformation of the limbs. These deficiencies need immediate treatment or permanent deformities can develop. Lack of calcium can lead to metabolic bone disease. When your turtle does not get enough calcium, the body steals calcium from the bones and shell, which causes them to weaken. The addition of supplements, increased exposure to ultraviolet light, and a diet with the proper phosphorous-to-calcium ratio are suggested treatments for this ailment.

VITAMIN POISONING

When it comes to your turtle's health, too much of a good thing can be very dangerous. Your pet needs vitamins A and D3 to stay healthy, but too much of either supplement can actually poison your turtle.

Excessive shedding of the skin is an indicator of vitamin A poisoning. Treat any wounds with a topical antibiotic and get your turtle to the veterinarian as soon as possible. Signs of vitamin D3 poisoning include softening of the shell and bleeding around the scutes. After you take your turtle to the veterinarian, you may have to provide more ultraviolet lighting. Avoid using vitamin A and vitamin D3 preparations if your turtle experiences poisoning, unless instructed otherwise by your veterinarian.

DIFFICULTY LAYING EGGS

If your female turtle experiences unproductive straining while trying to lay eggs, take your turtle to the veterinarian for treatment immediately. Mineral deficiencies, malformed eggs, or sand obstruction could be causing this problem. Only your veterinarian or herpetologist can determine the exact cause and treat your pet appropriately.

CARING FOR A SICK TURTLE

To ensure a sick turtle's speedy recovery, you should take several steps. If you have more than one turtle, you must quarantine the sick turtle as soon as possible to keep illnesses from spreading to the other turtles. Even if you have only one

turtle, you might want to quarantine a sick turtle. This allows you to keep your turtle's regular home sanitized in anticipation of the time when it is ready to return. Place the quarantine tank in a separate room, away from the turtle's regular home. Provide terrestrial turtles with a food dish, a water bowl, substrate, a hide box, and proper lighting. Aquatic turtles will need a very clean tank filled with water. This tank should also include a basking area and proper ultraviolet lighting. You may want to consider raising the temperature of the quarantine tank to the upper limit of your species' temperature recommendation. This could help boost the turtle's immune system.

Before placing your turtle in its temporary home, allow the turtle to bathe in a tub of warm water. This helps wash away any germs and contaminated dirt from the original tank. After allowing the turtle to soak for ten to twenty minutes, dry the turtle off and put it in its quarantine tank. Depending on the illness, you may have to quarantine your turtle for a few months. You veterinarian can recommend a suitable length of time for quarantine. During this period, it is important to keep a close eye on your turtle and record any changes in its appetite and behavior. Carefully examine your

If your turtle becomes sick, bathe him in a tub of warm water to wash away germs or bacteria, then follow your veterinarian's advice for treatment. Your sick turtle must be separated from your other turtles until he has a clean bill of health.

turtle's waste for worms and other intestinal parasites. You must also pay extra attention to your turtle's hygiene. Make sure your turtle's tank is clean, change the water daily, and remove uneaten food promptly. This will keep bacteria from building up around your turtle. Once your turtle seems to be its lively self again, you can prepare it for the move back home.

❧❧❧❧

The best medicine for all pets is prevention. The easiest way to guarantee your turtle's good health is to feed it a varied diet, make sure it gets enough exercise, and pay close attention to hygiene. If your turtle gets sick, remember that a trained veterinarian or herpetologist is always the best person to consult. Annual checkups with your turtle's veterinarian and proper care will keep your turtle happy and healthy.

CHAPTER EIGHT

Enjoying Your Pet

It is easy to gauge the happiness of a dog or cat—a content dog wags its tail and a happy cat purrs. It is not as easy for turtle owners to tell if their pets are happy. Turtles cannot vocalize their problems, so they resort to other behaviors when something bothers them. Some turtle behavior com-

pletely baffles their owners. The best way to tell if your turtle is happy and healthy is by observation. Watch your turtle carefully. This will help you understand what makes your turtle happy. Individual turtles behave differently, but a few behaviors are common to most species.

A turtle can make a fantastic pet, if you can learn to understand what his behaviors mean.

YOUR TURTLE WITHDRAWS INTO ITS SHELL

Turtles withdraw into their shells to protect themselves. This is an instinctive defense mechanism against faster predators. Do not feel hurt if your turtle withdraws into its shell when you attempt to handle it. This is a completely natural behavior. Work on earning your turtle's trust by using food rewards to help it understand that you are not a threat. Eventually, your turtle will come out of its shell while being handled.

YOUR TURTLE PACES

Pacing is an extremely common behavior, especially in terrestrial turtles. Turtles kept in glass terrariums are most likely looking for a way to escape. If your turtle is a new member of the family, it may need time to adjust to its surroundings. Consider putting a grate across the top of the terrarium in case your turtle starts to climb the walls. After a few days, see if your turtle's behavior has improved. When your turtle has calmed down, it has probably accepted its new home.

A turtle that continues to pace could have a problem with the home you have provided. Inspect the turtle's habitat to determine whether something is making it uncomfortable. Keep other animals out of the space where your turtle spends most of its time. A stressed turtle is likely to develop health problems, so it is best to find the source of the problem and deal with it accordingly.

YOUR TURTLE STRETCHES OUT ON ALL FOURS

If you spot your turtle lounging in the sunshine with all four of its arms and legs stretched out, it is probably just sunbathing. Turtles enjoy lots of light, especially during special trips outdoors. Carefully check any turtle that spends all its time in this position under a heat lamp or outside in the sunshine. From previous observation, you should be

Withdrawing into his shell is completely natural for a turtle. Don't take it personally! Perhaps he is frightened, cold, or just not feeling well.

able to tell if your turtle is less energetic than usual. If this is the case, take your turtle to the veterinarian as soon as possible.

YOUR TURTLE STANDS ON ITS HIND LEGS

Your turtle might stand up on its hind legs. There could be two reasons for this. First, your turtle could be curious about someone or something in the room. Your turtle's terrific sense of smell helps it recognize changes in its environment. If you have a treat with you, or if you have brought a friend over to meet your turtle, your turtle might be aware of this. Whatever it is, your turtle will be able to tell when something has changed and will be curious to see what is happening. Second, your turtle might also be defecating. Give your pet a little privacy and come back later to see how it is doing.

YOUR TURTLE HIDES AND REFUSES TO EAT

A turtle that hides or refuses to eat is most likely suffering from some sort of ailment. It is important for you to carefully inspect your turtle right away. Gently pick up your turtle to conduct a quick inspection. A turtle that appears listless or indifferent to handling is probably sick. If you do not notice any injuries that require your immediate attention, but you are still concerned, take your turtle to the veterinarian. Your turtle could be suffering from an illness.

Another reason some turtles exhibit this behavior is that they are ready to hibernate. Turtles kept in optimum climate conditions year-round may not need to hibernate. Other turtles are preprogrammed to hibernate. Depending on the species, you will have to provide your turtle with the materials it needs to hibernate for the colder winter months.

YOUR TURTLE OPENS ITS MOUTH WIDE

Turtles do not vocalize, so a wide-open mouth could mean that something is wrong. Listen carefully to see if you detect any wheezing. A turtle with a respiratory infection might be trying to draw in more air through its mouth. Take any noticeable change in breathing very seriously. This situation calls for a trip to the veterinarian. If your turtle is breathing normally but still has its mouth agape, inspect it carefully. The animal may have a physical injury. You might also look at your turtle's home. Perhaps something about its living quarters is upsetting the turtle.

YOUR TURTLES FIGHT

Turtles, especially aquatic ones, are extremely territorial. Male turtles housed in a home that is too small for several turtles to live in together harmoniously will fight. Mating can also prompt male turtles to spar to show off for females. Fighting can cause serious injuries.

If you want to keep more than one male turtle, consider housing them separately or purchasing a larger tank so they are less likely to fight. You might want to buy another tank specifically to separate males during mating season.

BREEDING YOUR TURTLE

As more species are captured or sold as pets, wild turtle populations decrease. For this reason, many turtle owners feel the desire to participate in captive breeding to ensure the survival of each species. Although some general rules apply to most turtles, sexual maturity and specific mating rituals will vary between species.

For most turtles, breeding begins in the spring and continues through the early fall. Many changes can trigger the urge to breed in both terrestrial and aquatic turtles. The seasonal

Because of their solitary nature, turtles are territorial animals. To prevent fighting, keep male turtles separated or in a large tank so each turtle has his own "space."

increase in temperature and the lengthening of the days during the summer months both contribute significantly to the urge to mate. If your turtles do not follow the natural disposition to hibernate each year, they may not be able to mate.

Because turtles are generally solitary creatures, many suspect that their keen sense of smell helps them find a mate across great distances. Scientists believe that higher temperatures can also increase the production of pheromones, allowing wild male turtles to track their mates from far away. In captivity, finding a mate is not so difficult.

Aquatic and terrestrial turtles mate differently. Aquatic turtles often engage in complex courtship rituals. The male attempts to woo the female while submerged in water. Using his long front claws, the male will stroke the face and forearms of the female. Breeders have also observed head bobbing in aquatic males while courting. If the female is ready and receptive, courtship will end and the mating process will begin. The turtles may remain submerged for several hours while they mate.

The courtship of terrestrial turtles is often much more aggressive. The male will render the female immobile by biting or nipping at its head, neck, or limbs. This encourages the female to draw its head and legs into the upper part of its shell. The male mounts the female from behind. If the female does not comply, the male may attempt to force itself on its intended mate by ramming their shells together. This can sometimes lead to serious injuries. If you wit-

MATING BEHAVIORS

If your turtles are mating, you might notice them sniffing each other. Turtles have a highly developed sense of smell. Male and female turtles will sniff each other during mating season to see if they are compatible. Different species have different odors. Turtles from closely related species can mate and have offspring. Many breeders, however, discourage owners from allowing this to happen. You should avoid crossbreeding to protect each species.

A female turtle that begins digging is ready to lay eggs. Once your turtle has laid its eggs, remove the eggs from the terrarium and place them in an incubation chamber.

Some species of turtles will deposit all their eggs at once, while others do so at intervals of five to thirty days. You should lightly number the eggs, using a pencil, to help you keep track.

ness behavior that you think could severely harm one or both of your turtles, separate the two of them for a few days before attempting to breed them again. Once the female accepts the male, it may produce hissing, grunting, or whistling noises.

Though aquatic and terrestrial turtles are very different in the ways they mate, all turtles need a suitable earthen nesting area in which to lay their eggs. Most females will dig a well-defined nest, so it is important for you to provide your turtle with a suitable amount of soil in which to dig. Depending on the species and its size, this may mean that your turtle will need a separate tank filled with soil to dig a nest.

The set of eggs your turtle produces is called the clutch. The number of eggs in a clutch will vary. Once the clutch is complete, your turtle will begin to cover the eggs with loose soil. When your turtle is finished, remove the eggs from the nest, and put them in an incubation chamber. The artificial chamber protects the eggs from turning and ensures that they remain in a climate-controlled environment.

You have several options when it comes to incubation chambers. Most pet stores sell incubators with a clear plastic lid, and you can fill the base with dampened builder's sand, which you can get from a hardware store. Bury the eggs halfway in the sand, and close the lid on the container. Place the container in a room where the temperature is consistently 82° F (28° C). Remove the lid every day to allow fresh air in. You should tilt one side of the container to avoid condensation buildup inside the lid and to allow moisture to run off the lid, away from the eggs.

If you are looking for something more precise, a homemade incubator might be the solution. Place two bricks vertically in the bottom of a large plastic terrarium. Fill the terrarium with water to just about the top of the bricks. Bury the eggs in a plastic container with moist builder's sand. Set the container on top of the two bricks. Make sure the container is secure and cannot tip over. Heat the water to about 82° F (28° C) with an aquarium heater. Place a pane of glass on top of the terrarium. Slightly tilt the glass so that any condensation can run off, away from the eggs.

The gestation period of turtles varies by species. Some species take up to 400 days to hatch! Hatchlings use an egg tooth to break out of their shells. It can take up to a day for the baby turtle to free itself completely. After the turtles emerge, you may notice large umbilical egg sacs attached to the hatchlings. These are usually absorbed in about two days. To keep the egg sacs from rupturing, you may want to place damp paper towels around the incubator until you move the turtles to their new tank. Your little turtles will not require food until the egg sacs have been completely absorbed. Provide the new turtles with fresh water and monitor their progress carefully over the next few days. When the egg sacs are gone, it is safe to introduce the hatchlings to their new home.

Separate baby turtles from any larger turtles you keep until the babies are at least one year old.

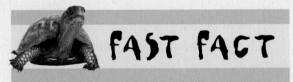

FAST FACT

The yolk of a turtle egg is large and could crush the embryo, so you should avoid turning turtle eggs after placing them in the incubator. Once the eggs are safely in the incubator, place the unit in a quiet, sheltered area where nothing will disturb it.

A baby box turtle emerges from his egg. Newborn turtles should be kept apart from older turtles until they are about a year old.

Because the newborns are so delicate, house them in a clean, stress-free environment to get them off to the best possible start. Depending on the species, your baby turtles will require the same sort of facilities as older turtles. They need the proper food, water, and lighting to grow into healthy adults. Remember that calcium is especially important to a hatchling's developing bones and

shell. Provide young turtles with supplements and a balanced diet to ward off any potential health problems.

TRAVELING WITH YOUR TURTLE

Turtles are creatures of habit, so traveling can be stressful for them. It is sometimes necessary to transport turtles to your veterinarian's office for checkups and emergencies. Aquatic turtles can be out of the water for short trips to the veterinarian. Put some damp paper towels in a cloth bag and then place your turtle inside. For longer trips, you may need to stop and provide your turtle with enough water to drink and cool off in.

Smaller terrestrial turtles can also be placed in cloth bags and then in cardboard boxes. Larger turtles might require wooden boxes. Make sure no rough edges could harm your turtle. Provide terrestrial turtles with fresh water on longer trips.

Turtles do not do well in unfamiliar environments. If you are planning a vacation, ask a friend or neighbor you trust to look after your turtle while you are away. Taking your turtle with you will present problems and stress your turtle. If you are breeding your turtles, it is best not to leave them in the care of a sitter during mating season. An inexperienced person would not understand how to care for a turtle that is ready to lay eggs. If your turtle is hibernating, explain normal hibernation behavior and anything your turtle sitter should be on the lookout for.

You should invite your turtle sitter over before your leave for vacation to show her where you keep your turtle's food and supplies. You should feed your turtle while your sitter is present to help the sitter understand your turtle's feeding routine. Explain

TURTLE SITTER CHECKLIST

Terrestrial Turtles' Water
- Provide fresh drinking water daily

Aquatic Turtles' Water
- Inspect the filter for problems
- Partially change the water in the tank after one week

Feeding Terrestrial Turtles
- Write down what you fed the turtle and how much food you provided
- Remove all uneaten food from the tank
- Write down which supplements you gave to the turtle and how often you provided them

Feeding Aquatic Turtles
- Write down what you fed the turtle and how much food you provided
- Feed aquatic turtles in separate feeding tanks to avoid contaminating the turtle's water
- Write down which supplements you gave to the turtle and how often you provided them

Equipment
- Make sure all lights, heaters, and filters are working properly

Behavior
- Note any unusual behavior
- If the turtle is hiding and refuses to eat, contact the veterinarian

how the turtle's tank is set up. Demonstrate how any devices, such as a water heater, work so your sitter will know how to make any necessary adjustments. Provide the sitter with contact information for you and your veterinarian in case of an emergency. You should also provide your sitter with a checklist. (See "Turtle Sitter Checklist," page 100.)

❧❧❧

Turtles are fascinating creatures that bring endless amounts of pleasure to their owners. Watching your turtle grow and thrive is a joyful experience. While interaction can be somewhat limited, observing turtle behavior on a daily basis is a treat that few people get to experience. Understanding your turtle and its needs is the best way to guarantee it has a long, happy, and healthy life.

Organizations to Contact

**Association of Reptilian and
Amphibian Veterinarians**
P.O. Box 605
Chester Heights, PA 19017
Phone: 610-358-9530
Fax: 610-892-4813
Email: ARAVETS@aol.com
Web site: www.arav.org

Chelonian Research Foundation
168 Goodrich St.
Lunenburg, MA 01462
Phone: 978-582-9668
Fax: 978-582-6279
Email: RhodinCRF@aol.com
Web site: www.chelonian.org

Desert Tortoise Council
P.O. Box 3273
Beaumont, CA 92223
Web site: www.deserttortoise.org

Endangered Habitats League
8424-A Santa Monica Blvd., No. 592
Los Angeles, CA 90069
Phone: 213-804-2750
Fax: 323-654-1931
Email: dsilverla@earthlink.net
Web site: www.ehleague.org/
   index.html

**National Save the Sea Turtle
Foundation**
4419 West Tradewinds Ave.
Ft. Lauderdale, FL 33308
Phone: 954-351-9333
Toll free: 877-TURTLE3
Fax: 954-351-5549
Email: nststf@bellsouth.net
Web site: www.savetheseaturtle.org

**National Wildlife Rehabilitators
Association (NWRA)**
2625 Clearwater Rd., Suite 110
St. Cloud, MN 56301
Phone: 320-230-9920
Fax: 320-230-3077
Email: NWRA@nwrawildlife.org
Web site: www.nwrawildlife.org

The Reptile Information Network
(Also Mid-Atlantic Reptile Show
[MARS] and MARS Reptile &
Amphibian Rescue)
P.O. Box 65012
Baltimore, MD 21209
Phone: 410-580-0250
Email: info@reptileinfo.com
Web site: www.reptileinfo.com

Save-A-Turtle
Jeri Sears, president
P.O. Box 361
Islamorada, FL 33036
Email: jermax22@yahoo.com
Web site: www.save-a-turtle.org

Sea Turtle Preservation Society
P.O. Box 510988-0988
Melbourne Beach, FL 32951
Phone: 321-676-1701
Email: stps@bellsouth.net
Web site: www.seaturtlespacecoast.org

Sea Turtle Restoration Project
P.O. Box 370
Forest Knolls, CA 94933
Phone: 415-663-8590
Fax: 415-663-9534
Email: info@seaturtles.org
Web site: www.seaturtles.org

Society for the Study of Amphibians and Reptiles
Marion Preest, Secretary
Joint Science Department
The Claremont Colleges
925 N. Mills Ave.
Claremont, CA 91711
Phone: 909-607-8014
Fax: 909-621-8588
Email: mpreest@jsd.claremont.edu
Web site: www.ssarherps.org

Tortoise Group
5157 Poncho Circle
Las Vegas, NV 89119
Phone: 702-739-7113
Fax: same as phone
Email: tortoisegroup@att.net
Web site: www.tortoisegroup.org

Tortoise Trust
BM Tortoise
London
WC1N 3XX
United Kingdom
Email: tortoisetrust@aol.com
Web site: www.tortoisetrust.org

Turtle Homes
P.O. Box 126
Okeechobee, FL 34973
Phone: 516-945-4098
Email: Marissa@turtlehomes.org
Web site: www.turtlehomes.org

Further Reading

Bartlett, R. D., and Patricia P. Bartlett. *Turtles and Tortoises: A Complete Pet Owner's Manual*. Hauppauge, NY: Barron's Educational, 1996.

Bartlett, R. D., and Patricia P. Bartlett. *Aquatic Turtles: Sliders, Cooters, Painted, and Map Turtles*. Hauppauge, NY: Barron's Educational, 2003.

Flank, Lenny, Jr. *Turtle*, 2nd ed. Hoboken, NJ: Wiley Publishing, 2007.

Girling, Simon, J. *Pet Owner's Guide to the Tortoise*. Surrey, UK: Ringpress Books, 2002.

Palika, Liz. *Turtles and Tortoises for Dummies*. New York: Hungry Minds, 2001.

Patterson, Jordan. *The Guide to Owning a Red-Eared Slider*. Neptune, NJ: TFH Publications, 1994.

Pritchard, Peter, C. H. *Encyclopedia of Turtles*. Neptune, NJ: TFH Publications, 1979.

de Vosjoli, Philippe. *Popular Tortoises*. Mission Viejo, CA: Advanced Vivarium Systems, 1996.

de Vosjoli, Philippe, and Roger Klingenberg. *The Box Turtle Manual*, 3rd ed. Irvine, CA: Advanced Vivarium Systems, 2003.

Wilke, Harmut. *Tortoises and Box Turtles: A Complete Pet Owner's Manual*. Translated by Celia Bohannon. Hauppauge, NY: Barron's Educational, 2000.

Internet Resources

www.aqua.org

The National Aquarium at Baltimore's Web site offers information about the conservation of all types of animals. The site also offers exhibits and information about the animals at the aquarium. The Reptile section of the Web site gives information about specific species of turtles.

www.chelonian.org

The Chelonian Research Foundation's Web site focuses on the conservation and preservation of the world's turtles. This Web site provides information about various turtle newsletters that offer important tips and statistics.

www.sandiegozoo.org

The San Diego Zoo's Web site is filled with information about conservation of animals and the benefits of being a member of this important zoo. The Animal Bytes portion of this site offers valuable information about turtles and tortoises. It gives general information about certain species. The Web site also features information about turtles' shells, diets, natural habitats, senses, and behaviors.

www.tortoisetrust.org

The Tortoise Trust Web site provides turtle owners with special updates and warnings about current herpetology problems. Tortoise Trust works to preserve and conserve turtles in the wild. Tortoise Trust also prepares new turtle owners for their pets and offers advice to keep turtle owners and their pets happy and healthy.

www.turtlecafe.com

Turtle Cafe sells food and supplements for turtles and tortoises to the public. The Web site tells turtle owners how to purchase specific supplements and foods that are important to a turtle's health and well-being. The Web site also offers advice and features articles about various topics dealing with captive turtles and tortoises.

www.worldwildlife.org

The World Wildlife Fund (WWF) is an important organization that helps raise awareness and money to protect endangered and threatened species. This site gives important information about the conservation of sea turtles. The Web site details how concerned turtle owners can get involved in these efforts.

Index

Numbers in **bold italics** refer to captions.

Contributors

MARIE DEVERS writes poetry, fiction, and nonfiction for young people and adults. As a senior editor at Northeast Editing, Inc., she creates educational content for students in grades K–12. An animal lover since childhood, she has cared for all sorts of pets, from turtles to monitor lizards to a hedgehog named Spike. She blogs about animals and pet care products on a Web site aimed at the owners of spoiled dogs. Marie has a degree in English from Saint Joseph's University and a master's degree from the University of Alaska Fairbanks. She lives in the Pocono Mountains of Pennsylvania with her husband, her chocolate lab, and two cats that love to lounge on her desk while she types.

Senior Consulting Editor **GARY KORSGAARD, DVM,** has had a long and distinguished career in veterinary medicine. After graduating from The Ohio State University's College of Veterinary Medicine in 1963, he spent two years as a captain in the Veterinary Corps of the U.S. Army. During that time he attended the Walter Reed Army Institute of Research and became Chief of the Veterinary Division for the Sixth Army Medical Laboratory at the Presidio, San Francisco.

In 1968 Dr. Korsgaard founded the Monte Vista Veterinary Hospital in Concord, California, where he practiced for 32 years as a small animal veterinarian. He is a past president of the Contra Costa Veterinary Association, and was one of the founding members of the Contra Costa Veterinary Emergency Clinic, serving as president and board member of that hospital for nearly 30 years.

Dr. Korsgaard retired in 2000, and currently enjoys golf, hiking, international travel, and spending time with his wife Susan and their three children and four grandchildren.